# INTRODUCTION

No matter how lovely his local stamping grounds, a countryman always likes exploring new ones. He'll grumble, of course, about the temporary upheaval ("What's to be done with the dog; who'll look after the horse?") but Britain is so rich in country sports and beautiful places in which to pursue them that he cannot resist for long. Then there's his town-based counterpart, pining for the chalkstream but tied by school fees, car insurance and a hundred other evils to an office five days a week.

This book offers help and ideas for everyone who loves the country. Full-time country dwellers will enjoy suggestions for fishing, shooting or hunting breaks around Britain – including many where the dog and horse can come too. And the rest of us will stay sane by planning sporting treats whenever we can escape our urban shackles, at the weekend, or tacked on to some obligatory errand. Why not take in the evening rise en route to a conference? Or slip off stalking after the end-of-term school pick-up?

Britain is peppered with inns and hotels with their own piece of water, stabling, or contacts with local shooting estates, and *The Field Guide To Sporting Hotels* lists 200 of them. Many have been visited and enjoyed by our staff and writers. Without succumbing to estate-agent waffle, this book provides all you need to know about sporting billets in England, Scotland, Wales and Ireland: what they cost, what sport they can provide, what they put in their nosebags, how to get there – and whether they welcome accompanying quadrupeds.

Compiled by the staff of *The Field*, the world's original country magazine, this book is an invaluable addition to any countryman's bookshelf or glove compartment. We hope you find many happy sporting days in it.

Lucy A Higginson

Deputy editor, *The Field*

## CONTENTS

Hartwell House, Oxford Road, Near Aylesbury, Buckinghamshire HP17 8NL
**Tel** 01296 747444 **Fax** 01296 747450
**e-mail** info@hartwell-house.com **website** www.hartwell-house.com
**Star ratings** ****AA Red; RAC Gold Ribbon

**NO OF ROOMS** 46.

**COST** From £215 per night bed and breakfast for a twin/double room. From £660 per night bed and breakfast for a suite.

**SPECIAL BREAKS/OFFERS** Please enquire. Summer and winter breaks available.

**FOOD** Fine dining. Fresh local produce used where possible. Extensive wine list. Awarded three AA rosettes.

**SPORT ON OFFER/THAT CAN BE ARRANGED** Trout fishing on hotel's own lake amid 90 acres of parkland. Also tennis and golf. Hunting with the Vale of Aylesbury, Old Berks and Bicester with Whaddon Chase.

**SEASONS/BEST TIMES FOR SPECIALIST SPORTS** Traditional seasons.

**DOGS/CHILDREN WELCOME** Dogs welcome in Hartwell Court. Children over eight-years-old.

**ANY OTHER INFO** Hartwell House, a Grade I listed building, used to be the private residence of the Lee and Hampden families. Luxurious country house hotel. Member of the Relais & Chateaux consortium. Indoor swimming pool, spa bath, steam room and sauna, gym and tennis courts.

**HOW TO GET THERE** From London: M40 junction 2 then A355 to Amersham then A413 to Aylesbury. Take A418 towards Oxford and the hotel is two miles on right. Or, M40 to junction 7 then A329/A418 toward Stone. Hotel is on the left after the village.

The Old Bridge Hotel, 1 High Street, Huntingdon, Cambridgeshire PE29 3TQ
**Tel** 01480 424300 **Fax** 01480 411017
**e-mail** oldbridge@huntsbridge.co.uk
**Star ratings** ***AA

**NO OF ROOMS** 25.

**COST** From £79.50 to £149.50 per person per night bed and breakfast.

**SPECIAL BREAKS/OFFERS** From £67.50 per person per night dinner, bed and breakfast sharing a double/twin room or from £82.50 per person per night dinner, bed and breakfast in a single room for a weekend break.

**FOOD** Large varied menu in the restaurant. More informal meals available on the terrace. Extensive wine list. Awarded two AA rosettes and the wine list is recommended by Egon Ronay.

**SPORT ON OFFER/THAT CAN BE ARRANGED** Fishing at Grafham Water. Local pheasant-shooting. Racing at Huntingdon and Newmarket. Watersports at Grafham Water. Boating trips along the Ouse from the hotel's private jetty. Golf and riding.

**SEASONS/BEST TIMES FOR SPECIALIST SPORTS** Traditional seasons, otherwise year round.

**DOGS/CHILDREN WELCOME** Children welcome. Well-behaved dogs welcome.

**ANY OTHER INFO** The Old Bridge is an 18th-century inn which previously acted as a private bank. It overlooks the River Ouse and is popular with the locals.

**HOW TO GET THERE** From the north: take A14/Cambridgeshire/M11 exit. Huntingdon is a mile later on left. From the south: Huntingdon is signposted from A14 just after it crosses A1. The Old Bridge Hotel is situated off the inner ring road immediately after the exit to Godmanchester and Cambridge.

La Grand Mare, Vazon Bay, Castel, Guernsey, Channel Islands GY5 7LL
**Tel** 01481 253544 **Fax** 01481 255194 **website** www.lgm.guernsey.net
**Star ratings** ****AA

**NO OF ROOMS** 35.

**COST** From £59 (low season) per person per night bed and breakfast based on two people sharing a double room. From £69 (high season) per person per night bed and breakfast based on two people sharing a double room.

**SPECIAL BREAKS/OFFERS** Please enquire.

**FOOD** Most of the hotel's vegetables, fruit and herbs grown on the island. Otherwise only the best fresh produce used. Rotisserie and pastry desserts are specialities. Conservatory offers lighter snacks. Exceptional wine list. Vintage ports and brandies on offer. Awarded two AA rosettes.

**SPORT ON OFFER/THAT CAN BE ARRANGED** Mirror carp, carp and perch fishing on the hotel's lake. Sea fishing. Clay pigeon shooting. Also golf, sailing, swimming, windsurfing, gym and health centre.

**SEASONS/BEST TIMES FOR SPECIALIST SPORTS** Traditional seasons.

**DOGS/CHILDREN WELCOME** No dogs. Children welcome.

**ANY OTHER INFO** La Grand Mare belongs to the Vermeulen family who built it over 20 years ago. The private grounds extend to over 110 acres. Beach. Handmade staircase and the bathrooms are tiled in exotic Italian tiles. Sauna and steam room. Hot spas.

**HOW TO GET THERE** By air or by sea from Poole.

Crabwall Manor Hotel, Parkgate Road, Mollington, Chester, Cheshire CH1 6NE
**Tel** 01244 851666 **Fax** 01244 851000
**e-mail** sales@crabwall.com **website** www.crabwall.com
**Star ratings** ****AA/RAC Blue Ribbon

**NO OF ROOMS** 48. Ground-floor bedroom suitable for disabled use.

**COST** From £125 per night bed and breakfast for a single room. From £150 per night bed and breakfast for a double room.

**SPECIAL BREAKS/OFFERS** Please enquire.

**FOOD** Traditional English and French cuisine. Extensive wine list with the hotel boasting separate red and white wine cellars. Juice bar in Spa. Awarded three AA rosettes.

**SPORT ON OFFER/THAT CAN BE ARRANGED** Clay pigeon shooting. Air-rifle shooting. Fishing in North Wales and Cheshire – please enquire. Also golf, crossbow, archery, riding, gym and ballooning. Racing from Chester, Haydock and Aintree.

**SEASONS/BEST TIMES FOR SPECIALIST SPORTS** Traditional seasons.

**DOGS/CHILDREN WELCOME** Only guide dogs. Children welcome.

**ANY OTHER INFO** The origins of Crabwall Manor began long before the Norman Conquest. The house, which is surrounded by 12 acres of grounds, has been refurbished by Laura Ashley designers. Previously it housed the Mayors of Chester and it also used to belong to the Jacob family (as in the crackers). Indoor swimming pool. Air-conditioned gym. Aerobics room. Beauty treatments. Billiards room. Licensed for weddings.

**HOW TO GET THERE** M6 to junction 20. M56 to Chester. At end of M56 follow signs to Queensferry and North Wales on A5117. Turn left on to A540 and hotel 2½ miles from Chester. From Liverpool: Take the Birkenhead Tunnel from central Liverpool for M53. M53 to junction 10. Turn right at roundabout on to A5117 to North Wales and Queensferry. Take A540 to Chester.

Fox & Hounds, Cotherstone, Barnard Castle, Co Durham DL12 9PF
**Tel** 01833 650241 **Fax** 01833 650241
**e-mail** mcarlisle@foxcotherstone.co.uk **website** www.foxcotherstone.co.uk
**Star ratings** ***AA/English Tourist Board

**NO OF ROOMS** 10.

**COST** From £37.50 per night bed and breakfast for a single room. From £55 per night bed and breakfast for a double room.

**SPECIAL BREAKS/OFFERS** Please enquire.

**FOOD** The bar and restaurant serve home-made food complemented by fine wines and a range of real ales. Only the finest and freshest ingredients used.

**SPORT ON OFFER/THAT CAN BE ARRANGED** Brown trout fishing on the Rivers Tees and Balder, as well as two well-stocked reservoirs. Sailing on Selset Reservoir. Livery stables nearby.

**SEASONS/BEST TIMES FOR SPECIALIST SPORTS** Traditional seasons.

**DOGS/CHILDREN WELCOME** Yes.

**ANY OTHER INFO** This traditional 200-year-old coaching inn, owned by Michael and May Carlisle, is situated yards from the banks of the River Tees. Features include beamed bar and log fires.

**HOW TO GET THERE** On B6277 four miles west of Barnard Castle.

The Manor House Inn, Carterway Heads, Shotley Bridge, Consett, County Durham DH8 9LX
**Tel** & **Fax** 01207 255268 **e-mail** manorhouseinn@aol.com
**Star ratings** Four AA Diamonds

**NO OF ROOMS** Four.

**COST** From £33 per night bed and breakfast for a single room. From £55 per night bed and breakfast for a double room. From £65 per night bed and breakfast for a family room.

**FOOD** All homemade from fresh, local produce. Moira Brown's homemade puddings and ice creams a speciality. Very extensive wine list. Selection of real ales including four guest ales and a cider. Awarded two AA rosettes. Recommended by *The Good Food Guide.*

**SPORT ON OFFER/THAT CAN BE ARRANGED** Local angling on Derwent Reservoir. Brown trout fishing on the River Derwent. Clay pigeon shooting.

**SEASONS/BEST TIMES FOR SPECIALIST SPORTS** Traditional seasons.

**DOGS/CHILDREN WELCOME** Yes.

**ANY OTHER INFO** The Manor House Inn has been owned and run by Chris and Moira Brown for three years. It is in a fairly remote location yet guests travel for miles to eat. Recommended by *The Good Pub Guide.*

**HOW TO GET THERE** On A68, seven miles south of Colbridge.

The Morritt Arms Hotel, Greta Bridge, Barnard Castle, County Durham DL12 9SE
**Tel** 01833 627232 **Fax** 01833 627392
**e-mail** relax@themorritt.co.uk **website** www.themorritt.co.uk
**Star ratings** ***AA

**NO OF ROOMS** 23.

**COST** From £59.50 per night bed and breakfast for a single room. From £79.50 per night for a standard double and from £89.50 per night for a superior double.

**SPECIAL BREAKS/OFFERS** From £72 per night for a single room to £104.50 per night for a double room dinner, bed and breakfast on the Dickens of a Break (minimum two-night stay).

**FOOD** The Copperfield Restaurant offers both table d'hôte and à la carte menus. Pallets Bistro and Dickens Bar. Award-winning wine list. Awarded an AA rosette.

**SPORT THAT CAN BE ARRANGED** Grouse-shooting on Bowes and Cotherstone moors, as well as Holwick estate. Local pheasant-, partridge- and woodcock-shooting. Clay pigeon shooting, 4x4 driving, golf and riding locally.

**SEASONS/BEST TIMES FOR SPECIALIST SPORTS** Traditional seasons.

**DOGS/CHILDREN WELCOME** Dogs welcome in standard rooms only, with their own bedding. Children under 12-years-old charged at £10 a night.

**ANY OTHER INFO** The Morritt gained its coaching-inn reputation through the Dickensian era as the second overnight stop for the London/Carlisle mail coach. Historic bar with famous Dickensian murals painted by John Gilroy.

**HOW TO GET THERE** North or south on the A1 to Scotch Corner, then west on the A66 for nine miles to Greta Bridge.

The Old Well Inn, 21 The Bank, Barnard Castle, Co Durham DL12 8PH
**Tel** 01833 690130 **Fax** 01833 690140
**Star ratings** Three English Tourist Board diamonds

**NO OF ROOMS** 10.

**COST** From £48 per night bed and breakfast for a single room. From £60 per night bed and breakfast for a double or family room.

**SPECIAL BREAKS/OFFERS** From £95 per person, dinner with a bottle of wine, bed and breakfast, for a two-night stay (Friday to Sunday).

**FOOD** All home made. Fresh fish and game in season. Gourmet nights and fish extravaganza evenings. Two restaurants – one is no smoking.

**SPORT ON OFFER/CAN BE ARRANGED** Driven grouse-shooting on Holwick and Wemmergill sporting estates, Bowes estate and Raby estate. Pigeon-shooting on Raby estate. Driven pheasant-shooting on Rokeby estate. Stalking on local estates.

**SEASONS/BEST TIMES FOR SPECIALIST SPORTS** 12 August to 1 February.

**DOGS/CHILDREN WELCOME** Children welcome; dogs by prior arrangement.

**ANY OTHER INFO** The Old Well, with gardens backing on to the massive outer Castle Wall, traces its existence as a hostelry to Tudor times when the extensive vaulted cellars served the needs of the townsfolk, travellers and soldiers. Not much has changed in that department. In fact, The Old Well was presented with *The Sunday Times*' Golden Pillow award in 1999. It also featured on BBC1's *Holidays Out* and BBC 2's *Food And Drink* programmes.

**HOW TO GET THERE** Barnard Castle is just off A66 trans-Pennine road linking A1 and M6. The Old Well is situated near to the top of The Bank, which is an extension of the main Market Place.

The Rose and Crown Hotel, Romaldkirk, Barnard Castle, County Durham DL12 9EB
**Tel** 01833 650213 **Fax** 01833 650828
**e-mail** hotel@rose-and-crown.co.uk **website** www.rose-and-crown.co.uk
**Star ratings** **AA/RAC

**NO OF ROOMS** 12.

**COST** From £62 per night bed and breakfast for a single room. From £86 per night bed and breakfast for a double/twin room.

**SPECIAL BREAKS/OFFERS** From £119 per person dinner, bed and breakfast for a two-night stay. This Teesdale Weekend Break runs from November to June, excluding Bank Holiday weekends.

**FOOD** Restaurant open each evening for dinner (except Sundays). Four-course, fixed-price menu costing £25 changes daily. Awarded two AA rosettes. Bar meals available lunch times and evenings.

**SPORT THAT CAN BE ARRANGED** Driven and walked-up grouse-shooting on Holwick and Wemmergill estates, Raby estate and Cotherstone moor. Partridge-shooting also available on Cotherstone moor and Raby estate where the latter also produces pheasants. Brown trout and salmon fishing available on the Strathmore stretch of the River Tees.

**SEASONS/BEST TIMES FOR SPECIALIST SPORTS** Traditional seasons.

**DOGS/CHILDREN WELCOME** Yes.

**ANY OTHER INFO** The Rose and Crown is an 18th-century coaching house. It has twice been named County Hotel of the Year by the *Which? Hotel Guide*. *The Good Pub Guide* has awarded this pub a star as well as naming it County Dining Pub of the Year 1998, 1999 and 2000.

**HOW TO GET THERE** Six miles north west of Barnard Castle on B6277 towards Middleton-in-Teesdale. Less than half an hour from A1 at Scotch Corner and under 45 minutes from Teeside Airport.

Halfway House, St Jidgey, Wadebridge, Cornwall PL27 7RE
**Tel** 01208 812524 **Fax** 01208 816571

**NO OF ROOMS** Four.

**COST** From £20 per person per night bed and breakfast.

**SPECIAL BREAKS/OFFERS** Please enquire.

**FOOD** A la carte. Steaks are a speciality.

**SPORT ON OFFER/THAT CAN BE ARRANGED** Game fishing on River Camel. Sea fishing either by boat or on shore from Padstow. Shark and wreck fishing aboard the Blue Fox with Phil Britts and Mike Turner. Foxhunting with Fourborrow or North Cornwall. Local game-shooting.

**SEASONS/BEST TIMES FOR SPECIALIST SPORTS** Traditional seasons.

**DOGS/CHILDREN WELCOME** Dogs welcome. Not really suitable for children.

**ANY OTHER INFO** Halfway House is a locally owned pub run by sporting owners Erica Simpson and Jim West.

**HOW TO GET THERE** On A39 between Wadebridge and St Columb.

Rose-In-Vale Country House Hotel, Mithian, St Agnes, Cornwall TR5 0QD
**Tel** 01872 552202 **Fax** 01872 552700
**e-mail** reception@rose-in-vale-hotel.co.uk **website** www.rose-in-vale-hotel.co.uk
**Star ratings** ***AA

**NO OF ROOMS** 18. Three ground-floor rooms suitable for the less able.

**COST** From £50.50 per night bed and breakfast for a single room. From £89 per night bed and breakfast for a double room.

**SPECIAL BREAKS/OFFERS** Please enquire.

**FOOD** Modern British/Continental. Cornish crab and lobster are specialities. Both table d'hôte and à la carte menus. Extensive and varied wine list based on 25 standard bins. Large selection of mainly French house wines and a choice of 10 wines for the more discerning palate. RAC Dining Award 1.

**SPORT ON OFFER/THAT CAN BE ARRANGED** Sea fishing from Falmouth, St Ives and Padstow. Watersports, sailing, tennis, swimming, gliding, golf, riding and power flying.

**SEASONS/BEST TIMES FOR SPECIALIST SPORTS** Traditional seasons.

**DOGS/CHILDREN WELCOME** Yes.

**ANY OTHER INFO** This is a very secluded and peaceful 18th-century manor house hotel set within its own 11-acre valley of gardens, woodland and pasture. Anthony and Vanda Arthur have owned it for 16 years. Originally, in the 1760s, it was built for Captain Oates who was the tin mine manager for this area. This was his winter residence – when the coastal gales were too much for him at his summer house, he retired to this sheltered valley. Outdoor swimming pool. Recommended by *The Good Hotel Guide* and Ashley Courtenay.

**HOW TO GET THERE** A30 through Cornwall. Two miles beyond Zelah village turn right on to B3284. Cross A3075. Take the third turning on the left to the hotel.

St Martin's On The Isle, St Martin's, Isles of Scilly TR25 0QW
**Tel** 01720 422092 **Fax** 01720 422298
**e-mail** stay@stmartinshotel.co.uk **website** www.stmartinshotel.co.uk
**Star ratings** ***AA

**NO OF ROOMS** 30.

**COST** From £85 per night dinner, bed and breakfast for a single room. From £175 per night dinner, bed and breakfast for a deluxe double. Price dependent on the season and whether the room has a garden or sea view.

**SPECIAL BREAKS/OFFERS** Please enquire.

**FOOD** Lunch served in the Round Island Bar. Dinner in the Teän Restaurant. Varied and extensive menu. Seafood a speciality. Awarded three AA rosettes and four RAC dining awards.

**SPORT ON OFFER/THAT CAN BE ARRANGED** Scuba diving, seal snorkelling, golf and sailing. Offshore fishing for mackerel and shark. Also cricket, tennis, windsurfing, swimming and cycling.

**SEASONS/BEST TIMES FOR SPECIALIST SPORTS** Traditional seasons.

**DOGS/CHILDREN WELCOME** Dogs charged at £12 per night. Children under 16-years-old free of charge when sharing with adults. Breakfast and high tea charged at £15 per day.

**ANY OTHER INFO** Surrounded by white sandy beaches. Launches leave the hotel daily for trips to other inhabited or uninhabited islands. Trips to the Eastern Isles to see the Atlantic grey seals. Indoor swimming pool. Local tennis court.

**HOW TO GET THERE** Skybus from Lands End, Newquay, Plymouth, Exeter and Bristol. *Scillonian III* from Penzance. Helicopter from Penzance. All to St Mary's. From there catch the *Voyager* or *Enterprise* boats to St Martin's.

The Budock Vean Hotel, The Hotel on the River, Helford River, Mawnan Smith, Falmouth, Cornwall TR11 5LG
**Tel** 01326 250288 **Fax** 01326 250892
**e-mail** relax@budockvean.co.uk **website** www.budockvean.co.uk
**Star ratings** ****AA

**NO OF ROOMS** 57.

**COST** From £49 per person per night bed and breakfast in either a single or double room.

**SPECIAL BREAKS/OFFERS** If guests book a four-night stay they can visit the gardens of Cornwall free of charge. Also gourmet weekends, golf workshops and shooting breaks.

**FOOD** Seafood a speciality. Otherwise fresh local produce used. Awarded two AA rosettes.

**SPORT ON OFFER/THAT CAN BE ARRANGED** The hotel has its own foreshore for sea fishing. Fly-fishing for brown and rainbow trout on Lake Stithians. Driven pheasant- and partridge-shooting at Penhardgard Barton farm, Helland. Also golf, sailing, tennis, swimming and archery.

**SEASONS/BEST TIMES FOR SPECIALIST SPORTS** Traditional seasons.

**DOGS/CHILDREN WELCOME** Dogs welcome. The hotel is not actively promoted to families with young children.

**ANY OTHER INFO** Budock Vean Hotel is set within 65 acres of award-winning valley gardens on the banks of the River Helford. Riverside sun lounge and private foreshore. Indoor swimming pool. Also has natural health spa specialising in reflexology, aromatherapy and massage.

**HOW TO GET THERE** Follow A39 to Falmouth. At the Hill Head roundabout turn right and follow signs for Trebah/Glendurgan gardens. Budock Vean Hotel is on the left-hand side half a mile after Trebah Gardens.

The Cornish Arms at Pendoggett, Port Isaac, Cornwall PL30 3HH
**Tel** 01208 880263 **Fax** 01208 880335 **e-mail** cornisharm@aol.com
**Star ratings** **AA

**NO OF ROOMS** Eight.

**COST** From £39 per night bed and breakfast for a single. From £59 per night bed and breakfast for a double room.

**SPECIAL BREAKS/OFFERS**
From £37.95 per person dinner, bed and breakfast (minimum two-night stay).

**FOOD** Restaurant specialises in fresh produce and locally caught fish. Also bar snacks. Well known for its real ale.

**SPORT ON OFFER/THAT CAN BE ARRANGED** Sea fishing from Rock and Padstow. Pheasant-shooting and clay pigeon shooting locally. Sailing from Rock. Water-skiing and golf.

**SEASONS/BEST TIMES FOR SPECIALIST SPORTS** Traditional seasons.

**DOGS/CHILDREN WELCOME** Yes.

**ANY OTHER INFO** The Cornish Arms is a 16th-century coaching inn featuring beams, slate floors and log fires.

**HOW TO GET THERE** Take A30 to Launceston, follow signs to Camelford on B3314. Go through Delabole. Five miles later The Cornish Arms is on the right.

The Jubilee Inn, Pelynt, Near Looe, Cornwall PL13 2JZ
**Tel** 01503 220312 **Fax** 01503 220920 **e-mail** rickard@jubileeinn.freeserve.co.uk
**Star ratings** **AA

**NO OF ROOMS** 11.

**COST** From £32.50 per person per night bed and breakfast based on two people sharing a double room.

**SPECIAL BREAKS/OFFERS** From £75 per person based on two sharing a double room for a three-night stay.

**FOOD** Both bar and à la carte meals. Extensive and varied menus with emphasis on crab, lobster, scallops, mackerel, sole, plaice and cod. Fine selection of real ales. Extensive wine list.

**SPORT ON OFFER/THAT CAN BE ARRANGED** Deep sea fishing from Fowey and Looe. Carp fishing at Shilla Mill. Sailing and golf.

**SEASONS/BEST TIMES FOR SPECIALIST SPORTS** May to September.

**DOGS/CHILDREN WELCOME** Dogs charged £3.50 per day. Children welcome.

**ANY OTHER INFO** This pub's name was changed in 1887 from The Axe to celebrate the first 50 years of Queen Victoria's reign. It is owned by Gary and Veronica Rickard who are both local and took over the pub in 1998. There is a spiral staircase designed by Stuart Armfield, the well-known West Country artist, as well as many of his paintings and watercolours on the pub's walls.

**HOW TO GET THERE** M5, A30, A38, B3359. Pelynt is four miles from Looe, three miles from Polperro and five miles from Fowey.

The Old Success Inn, Sennen Cove, Land's End, Cornwall TR19 7DG
**Tel** 01736 871232 **Fax** 01736 871457
**Star ratings** **AA/English Tourist Board

**NO OF ROOMS** 12.

**COST** From £38 per person per night bed and breakfast based on two people sharing a double room.

**SPECIAL BREAKS/OFFERS** From £60 dinner, bed and breakfast for two people from the end of October to April.

**FOOD** Both bar and à la carte restaurant menus. Fresh local produce, especially seafood. Sunday lunch very popular.

**SPORT ON OFFER/THAT CAN BE ARRANGED** Sea fishing at St Ives. Also surfing, riding, cycling, golf and swimming.

**SEASONS/BEST TIMES FOR SPECIALIST SPORTS** Traditional seasons.

**DOGS/CHILDREN WELCOME** Yes.

**ANY OTHER INFO** The Old Success Inn lies in one of Cornwall's most beautiful bays. It is a 17th-century fisherman's inn, which has been attractively modernised and which is very popular with the locals.

**HOW TO GET THERE** A30 towards Penzance then follow the bypass for Land's End. After nine miles turn right by Sennen school to the foot of the cove.

Tredethy House, Helland Bridge, Bodmin, Cornwall, PL30 4QS
**Tel** 01208 841262 **Fax** 01208 841707
**e-mail** amandarose@tredethyhouse.co.uk **website** www.tredethyhouse.co.uk

**NO OF ROOMS** 15. Disable room available.

**COST** From £90 to £150 per night bed, breakfast and afternoon tea for a double room.

**SPECIAL BREAKS/OFFERS** Please enquire.

**FOOD** Home produce using fresh local products. Comprehensive and varied wine list.

**SPORT ON OFFER/THAT CAN BE ARRANGED** Coarse fishing locally. Sea fishing. Also riding, golf, cycling, swimming and watersports. Pheasant-shooting on a local estate.

**SEASONS/BEST TIMES FOR SPECIALIST SPORTS** Traditional seasons.

**DOGS/CHILDREN WELCOME** Dogs charged at £4 a day. Children welcome.

**ANY OTHER INFO** Tredethy is a Victorian mansion set within its own gardens overlooking the Camel valley. Previously it was owned by Prince Chula of Thailand who, with his cousin Prince Bira as driver, made up the famous Thirties motor racing team. Furnishings reflect the owner, Amanda Rose's travels. Guests will recognise the influence of many years spent in Africa as well as travels to China, Thailand and the Seychelles. Nine acres of woodlands and gardens. Children's lounge. Outdoor swimming pool.

**HOW TO GET THERE** Launceston A30. Turn to Helland before Bodmin. Hotel on left-hand side after Helland Bridge.

Crosby Lodge, High Crosby, Crosby-on-Eden, Carlisle, Cumbria CA6 4QZ
**Tel** 01228 573618 **Fax** 01228 573428
**e-mail** crosbylodge@crosby-eden.demon.co.uk **website** www.crosbylodge.co.uk
**Star ratings** ***AA and English Tourist Board Silver Award.

**NO OF ROOMS** 11.

**COST** From £82 per night bed and breakfast for a single room. From £110 per night bed and breakfast for a double/twin room.

**SPECIAL BREAKS/OFFERS** From £145 per person dinner (table d'hôte menu), bed and breakfast staying Friday and Saturday nights from October to end of March in twin/double room.

**FOOD** Traditional and continental cuisine prepared with fresh local produce. Seafood, game, home-made desserts and bread are specialities. Extensive wine list. Awarded an AA rosette for food.

**SPORT THAT CAN BE ARRANGED** Grouse-, pheasant- and partridge-shooting on the Whitfield estate and nearby estates. Salmon and brown trout fishing on the River Eden. Tuition can also be arranged higher up the River Eden near Lazonby.

**SEASONS/BEST TIMES FOR SPECIALISED SPORTS** Grouse: August and September. Partridge: September and October. Pheasant: November, December and January.

**DOGS/CHILDREN WELCOME** By prior arrangement.

**ANY OTHER INFO** Crosby Lodge has been owned and run by the Sedgwick family for 29 years. Son James is head chef and daughter Philippa is in charge of the wine cellar.

**HOW TO GET THERE** Leave M6 at junction 44. Follow signs for Brampton. The hotel is 3½ miles just off A689 at High Crosby.

Dale Head Hall Lakeside Hotel, Lake Thirlmere, Keswick, Cumbria CA12 4TN
**Tel** 01768 772478 **Fax** 01768 771070
**e-mail** enquiry@dale-head-hall.co.uk **website** www.dale-head-hall.co.uk
**Star ratings** ***AA

**NO OF ROOMS** 12.

**COST** From £33.50 per person per night bed and breakfast.

**SPECIAL BREAKS/OFFERS** From £50 per person per night dinner, bed and breakfast (minimum three-night stay). This offer is available all year; other offers on request.

**FOOD** Modern British. Awarded two AA red rosettes; ***RAC Restaurant award.

**SPORT ON OFFER/THAT CAN BE ARRANGED** Pike and fly-fishing for wild brown trout on Lake Thirlmere. Salmon fishing around Moffat and Tebay. Foxhunting with the Blencathra. Also golf.

**SEASONS/BEST TIMES FOR SPECIALIST SPORTS** Traditional seasons.

**DOGS/CHILDREN WELCOME** No dogs. Children over 10-years-old welcome in the restaurant for dinner. Four- to 14-year-olds charged £15 per night, 15 years and over £20 per night.

**ANY OTHER INFO** The Leathes family lived at Dale Head Hall for nearly 300 years. After the last of the family died out, Manchester Corporation bought the lake and hall to provide Victorian Manchester with clean drinking water and its successive mayors with an idyllic summer retreat. Now Alan and Shirley Lowe live at Dale Head Hall and run the hotel. Recommended by Johansens.

**HOW TO GET THERE** Thirlmere is situated midway between Keswick and Grasmere. Accessible from M6 using junction 36 and taking A591 north or by junction 40 and following A66 then B5322 on to A591. From there a quarter of a mile of private drive leads to the hall and lake.

Greenhead Hotel, Greenhead, Brampton, Cumbria CA8 7HB
**Tel** & **Fax** 01697 747411
**Star ratings** Three Diamonds English Tourist Board

**NO OF ROOMS** Four.

**COST** From £30 per person per night bed and breakfast for single room. From £22.50 per person per night bed and breakfast for a twin/double based on two people sharing.

**SPECIAL BREAKS/OFFERS** Please enquire.

**FOOD** Traditional English with emphasis on bar menus – especially steaks.

**SPORT ON OFFER/THAT CAN BE ARRANGED** Salmon, sea-trout and brown trout fishing conditions vary considerably within the area. Day tickets are available on the River Tyne. Very seasonal salmon and sea-trout fishing on the River Lynne, a small spate river flowing into the Solway Firth only 12 miles from the sea. Pheasant-shooting parties can be arranged at the neighbouring Blenkinsop estate. Roe deer stalking and golf.

**SEASONS/BEST TIMES FOR SPECIALIST SPORTS** Due to the range of river systems in this area it is best to speak direct with the proprietor Tom Goundry.

**DOGS/CHILDREN WELCOME** Yes.

**ANY OTHER INFO** The Greenhead Hotel is the local inn of the village of Greenhead which has a population of about 30 people. The Pennine Way and Roman wall pass straight through the village. The golf course is about 100yd from the hotel.

**HOW TO GET THERE** Half a mile off A69 Newcastle to Carlisle road.

Kirkstile Inn, Loweswater, Cockermouth, Cumbria CA13 0RU
**Tel** 01900 85219 **Fax** 01900 85239 **e-mail** kirkstileinn@aol.com
**Star ratings** Two Diamonds

**NO OF ROOMS** 15.

**COST** From £45 to £63 per person per night bed and breakfast.

**SPECIAL BREAKS/OFFERS** There is a 10 per cent discount on stays over four days.

**FOOD** Bar meals and four-course evening menu.

**SPORT ON OFFER/THAT CAN BE ARRANGED** Hunting with the Melbrake Hunt (foot pack). Brown trout fishing can be arranged with a local farmer on Lake Loweswater. High- and low-level walking. Also riding, climbing, boating, tennis and golf.

**SEASONS/BEST TIMES FOR SPECIALIST SPORTS** Traditional seasons.

**DOGS/CHILDREN WELCOME** Dogs charged at £3 a night. Children welcome.

**ANY OTHER INFO** This 16th-century pub is a favourite with the locals and it hosts meets and other functions for the Melbrake Foxhounds. It is renowned for its spontaneous singsongs, friendly hospitality and games of shove ha'penny.

**HOW TO GET THERE** Exit M6 at junction 40. Take A66 and follow signs to Keswick. Stay on A66 out of Keswick to Cockermouth. After two miles turn left to Braithwaite. Take the road for Lorton via the Whinlatter Pass. Drop down into Lorton and turn left to Buttermere. At the T-junction turn left to Loweswater/Buttermere. Follow this road and by the telephone box turn left to the Kirkstile Inn.

Lindeth Howe Country House Hotel, Lindeth Drive, Longtail Hill, Bowness on Windermere, Cumbria LA23 3JF
**Tel** 01539 445759 **Fax** 01539 446368
**e-mail** lindeth.howe@lakes-pages.co.uk **website** www.lakes-pages.co.uk
**Star ratings** ***AA/***Silver Award English Tourism Council

**NO OF ROOMS** 36. Two ground-floor rooms.

**COST** From £42.50 to £72.50 per person per night bed and breakfast.

**SPECIAL BREAKS/OFFERS** Vary, but there are reductions for longer stays. Please enquire.

**FOOD** Contemporary British. Wide selection of malt whiskies. No-smoking restaurant. Children under seven-years-old not allowed in dining room after 6.30pm but there is a high tea available from 5.30pm to 6pm.

**SPORT ON OFFER/THAT CAN BE ARRANGED** The hotel is a member of Windermere, Ambleside and District Angling Association. This allows free fly-fishing for brown trout on Dubbs and Ghyll Head Reservoirs as well as at Hayeswater, High Arnside, High Newton, Moss Eccles and School Knott. The hotel has its own indoor swimming pool. Golf, watersports, riding and climbing available locally. Livery stables nearby.

**SEASONS/BEST TIMES FOR SPECIALIST SPORTS** March to October.

**DOGS/CHILDREN WELCOME** No dogs in the hotel. Children welcome. Cots £8 per night; two- to six-year olds £19.75 bed and breakfast; seven to 14-year-olds are charged at 50 per cent of the adult price.

**ANY OTHER INFO** Lindeth Howe is set in six acres of mature grounds. It commands impressive views over Windermere, England's largest lake. The hotel was originally built for a wealthy mill owner who rented it out for holidays to friends, among them Beatrix Potter. It was here, between 1905 and 1913, that she wrote and illustrated several of her books. Eventually Potter bought the house for her mother. The hotel also has a sauna, solarium, drying and storage rooms.

**HOW TO GET THERE** Lindeth Howe is approximately 20 minutes' drive from M6 and one mile south of Bowness on Windermere. Leave M6 at J36 and proceed along A591 for eight miles, turning left at the roundabout on to B5284 signed to Hawkshead/Ferry and Crook. After seven miles the road crosses the Lyth Valley road on to Longtail Hill.

Lowbyer Manor Country House Hotel, Alston, North Pennines, Cumbria CA9 3JX
**Tel** 01434 381230 **Fax** 01434 382937 **website** www.lowbyermanor.ntb.org.uk
**Star ratings** **AA/RAC; **English Tourist Council

**NO OF ROOMS** 12.

**COST** From £36 per night bed and breakfast for a single room. From £72 per night bed and breakfast for a double room.

**SPECIAL BREAKS/OFFERS** From £89.50 per night dinner, bed and breakfast for a double room (minimum two-night stay). Christmas and New Year packages available later in year. Please enquire.

**FOOD** A la carte. Several vegetarian options. Other special diets by arrangement. Licence restricted to guests and visiting diners only so no public bar. Extensive wine list.

**SPORT ON OFFER/THAT CAN BE ARRANGED** The hotel can arrange grouse- and pheasant-shooting on moors in Alston and Whitfield. Shooting is also available in Teesdale and Weardale. Salmon and brown trout fly-fishing on the Rivers Tyne, North Tyne and Upper Tyne near Kielder Water. Stillwater fishing available locally. Also golf and riding.

**SEASONS/BEST TIMES FOR SPECIALIST SPORTS** Traditional seasons.

**DOGS/CHILDREN WELCOME** Yes.

**ANY OTHER INFO** Lowbyer Manor is a family-run hotel owned by Peter and Margaret Hughes, and was once owned by the Earl of Derwentwater. Drying facilities.

**HOW TO GET THERE** From M6 take A686 or A689 (depending which junction you leave the motorway) to Alston.

Nanny Brow Country House Hotel, Near Ambleside, Cumbria LA22 9NF
**Tel** 015394 32036 **Fax** 015394 32450
**e-mail** reservations@nanny brow.co.uk **website** www.nannybrow.co.uk
**Star ratings** ***AA

**NO OF ROOMS** 18.

**COST** From £65 per person per night dinner, bed and breakfast for a single or double room.

**SPECIAL BREAKS/OFFERS** From £169 per person dinner, bed and breakfast for a three-day break. From £194 per person dinner, bed and breakfast for a four-day break.

**FOOD** Modern English cuisine with most ingredients sourced locally. A speciality is the Nanny Brow lamb which is from Carol Fletcher's flock of Romneys. Extensive wine list. Awarded two AA rosettes.

**SPORT ON OFFER/THAT CAN BE ARRANGED** Fishing on the hotel's own stretch of the River Brathay and at Hawkshead Trout Farm. Pheasant- and grouse-shooting on local estates. Also sailing, watersports and golf.

**SEASONS/BEST TIMES FOR SPECIALIST SPORTS** Traditional seasons.

**DOGS/CHILDREN WELCOME** Dogs charged at £5 per night. Children welcome.

**ANY OTHER INFO** In 1902 this country house was designed by a London architect for his own use. It remained a family house until 1952 when it was converted to a hotel. It is now owned and run by Michael and Carol Fletcher. Nanny Brow sits under Loughrigg Fell within five acres of gardens and woodland. Recommended by Johansens. Also a four-bedroomed house to let.

**HOW TO GET THERE** M6 to junction 36. A591 to Ambleside then A593 to Coniston. Hotel 1½ miles outside Ambleside.

Tarn End House Hotel, Talkin Tarn, Brampton, Cumbria CA8 1LS
**Tel** 01697 72340 **Fax** 01697 72089
**Star ratings** **AA

**NO OF ROOMS** Seven.

**COST** From £74 per night bed and breakfast for a double room.

**SPECIAL BREAKS/OFFERS** From £61.50 to £68.50 per night bed and breakfast for a double room, or from £89.50 to £96.50 per night dinner, bed and breakfast for a double room (minimum two-night stay).

**FOOD** Modern European with traditional British influence. All food is produced on site using local produce. Meringues are a speciality.

**SPORT THAT CAN BE ARRANGED** Local coarse fishing on Talkin Tarn with daily permits. The hotel can also arrange grouse-shooting on the moors around Hexham as well as local pheasant-shooting. Also sailing, windsurfing and rowing on the Tarn. Golf locally.

**SEASONS/BEST TIMES FOR SPECIALIST SPORTS** Traditional seasons.

**DOGS/CHILDREN WELCOME** Yes.

**ANY OTHER INFO** Tarn End House, a former estate farm, is a family-run hotel resting in its own grounds with lawns running down to the shores of Talkin Tarn. Public rooms and most of the bedrooms overlook Talkin Tarn. The hotel is locally renowned for its good food.

**HOW TO GET THERE** From M6 take junction 43 and head east on A69 to Brampton. Go south on B6413 and turn left at the Talkin sign.

Temple Sowerby House Hotel, Temple Sowerby, Penrith, Cumbria CA10 1RZ
**Tel** 0800 146157 **Fax** 017683 61958
**e-mail** stay@temple-sowerby.com **website** www.temple-sowerby.com
**Star ratings** ***AA

**NO OF ROOMS** 13. Two rooms wheelchair accessible.

**COST** From £68 per night bed and breakfast for a single room. From £96 per night bed and breakfast for a double room.

**SPECIAL BREAKS/OFFERS** From £60 per person per night dinner, bed and breakfast in a double room based on two people sharing (minimum two-night stay).

**FOOD** English and Continental cuisine with traditional sauces. One AA rosette awarded.

**SPORT THAT CAN BE ARRANGED** Brown trout fishing on the River Eden. Stalking on the Lowther estate which also organises local pheasant- and grouse-shooting.

**SEASONS/BEST TIMES FOR SPECIALIST SPORTS** Shooting: 12 August to 31 January. Fishing: 15 March to 15 October.

**DOGS/CHILDREN WELCOME** Yes.

**ANY OTHER INFO** Temple Sowerby House Hotel is a former Cumbrian farmhouse with Georgian additions. It stands within its own two acres of walled gardens and overlooks Cross Fell, the highest peak in the Pennines.

**HOW TO GET THERE** Take M6 to junction 40. Take A66 and follow signs for Brough and Scotch Corner. The hotel is at Temple Sowerby.

The Blacksmiths Arms, Talkin Village, Brampton, Cumbria CA8 1LE
**Tel** 01697 73452 **Fax** 01697 73396
**Star ratings** AA Three Diamonds

**NO OF ROOMS** Five.

**COST** From £30 per person per night bed and breakfast in a single room. From £22.50 per person per night bed and breakfast in a double/twin room based on two people sharing.

**FOOD** Large and varied menu for both restaurant and bar based on home-cooked fresh local produce. Extensive wine list with 50 bins on offer. Three cask ales and a selection malt whiskies and eight gins.

**SPORT ON OFFER/THAT CAN BE ARRANGED** Pheasant- and grouse-shooting locally. Salmon fishing on the River Eden. Golf locally.

**SEASONS/BEST TIMES FOR SPECIALIST SPORTS** Traditional seasons.

**DOGS/CHILDREN WELCOME** No dogs. Children welcome.

**ANY OTHER INFO** Donald and Anne Jackson run this traditional country inn and daughter Emma helps with the cooking.

**HOW TO GET THERE** Take M6 to junction 43. Take A69 seven miles east to the roundabout and follow signs to Talkin Tarn Golf Club. Then follow signs for Talkin village after the level crossing.

The Miller Howe Hotel, Windermere, Cumbria LA23 1EY
**Tel** 01539 442536 **Fax** 01539 445664
**e-mail** lakeview@millerhowe.com **website** www.millerhowe.com
**star ratings** **AA Red

**NO OF ROOMS** 12.

**COST** From £63 per person per night dinner, bed and breakfast based on two people sharing.

**SPECIAL BREAKS/OFFERS** Mid-week offers, cookery courses and December offers. Please enquire.

**FOOD** Modern English gourmet cuisine. Over 250 wines on offer. Awarded two AA rosettes. *The Good Food Guide* Restaurant of the Year 1998.

**SPORT ON OFFER/THAT CAN BE ARRANGED** Brown and rainbow trout fishing on Lake Windermere and Ghyll Head Reservoir. Also riding, watersports, ballooning and golf.

**SEASONS/BEST TIMES FOR SPECIALIST SPORTS** Fishing: April to October.

**DOGS/CHILDREN WELCOME** Dogs welcome and charged £3 a night. No children under eight-years-old.

**ANY OTHER INFO** Miller Howe is an Edwardian house set within its own 4½ acres of landscaped gardens which reach down to Lake Windermere. It is run by Charles Gardside, former editor-in-chief of *The European*. The hotel was founded in 1971 by chef patron John Tovey and is today furnished with antiques, objets d'art, china and porcelain.

**HOW TO GET THERE** The hotel is on A592 between Windermere and Bowness. From the south: leave M6 at junction 36. Follow A591 past Windermere and turn left at roundabout towards Bowness on A592. From the north: leave M6 at junction 40. Follow A592 along Ullswater and over the Kirkstone Pass. Continue to Bowness on A592.

Trout Hotel, Crown Street, Cockermouth, Cumbria CA13 0EJ
**Tel** 01900 823591 **Fax** 01900 827514
**e-mail** enquiries@trouthotel.co.uk **website** www.trouthotel.co.uk
**Star ratings** ***AA/English Tourist Board highly recommended

**NO OF ROOMS** 29.

**COST** From £59.95 per night bed and breakfast for a single room. From £89.95 per night bed and breakfast for a double room. Junior suite from £129 per night bed and breakfast.

**SPECIAL BREAKS/ OFFERS** From £109.95 per person for a weekend break (two nights) dinner, bed and breakfast. From £127.50 per person for a fishing course with a qualified instructor over two nights with dinner, bed and breakfast.

**FOOD** Both à la carte and table d'hôte menus on offer emphasising local produce, notably beef, salmon and trout. Vegetarian meals available and special diets can be catered for with prior notice. Extensive and varied wine list. Awarded one AA rosette.

**SPORT ON OFFER/THAT CAN BE ARRANGED** Residents have access to salmon and brown trout fishing on the River Derwent from the hotel. Salmon and brown trout fishing courses available through The North of England School of Game Angling with qualified instructors for all levels on local beats of the River Derwent. Pheasant-shooting arranged by the hotel at the nearby Dovenby shoot. Also riding, cycling and sailing.

**SEASONS/BEST TIMES FOR SPECIALIST SPORTS** Fishing: February to July.

**DOGS/CHILDREN WELCOME** Dogs charged £5 a night. Children welcome.

**ANY OTHER INFO** The Trout, which looks out on to the banks of the River Derwent, was originally a private residence on the Egremont estate. It established itself as a fishing haven during the Sixties when the Rivers Derwent and Cocker were recognised for their excellent trout and salmon fishing. In 1995 The Trout was awarded the Glenmorangie Game Fishing Hotel of the Year. The extensive gardens achieved recognition by winning Cumbria in Bloom in 1989 and 1996.

**HOW TO GET THERE** From Carlisle, follow A595 direct to Cockermouth. From M6, leave at junction 40 and follow A66 direct to Cockermouth.

Tufton Arms Hotel, Market Square, Appleby-in-Westmorland, Cumbria CA16 6XA
**Tel** 017683 51593 **Fax** 017683 52761
**e-mail** info@fishing-shooting.co.uk **website** www.fishing-shooting.co.uk
**Star ratings** ***AA

**NO OF ROOMS** 21.

**COST** From £55 per night bed and breakfast for a single room or £90 per night bed and breakfast for a double room.

**SPECIAL BREAKS/OFFERS** From £110 per person dinner, bed and breakfast for a Winter Break (minimum two-night stay). Third night free with only dinner to pay for. Fly-fishing course includes four nights' dinner, bed and breakfast for £465 per person.

**FOOD** All 211 dishes prepared using fresh local produce. There is a wine list of over 160 bins. Awarded an AA red rosette and an RAC restaurant merit. Bar meals also available.

**SPORT ON OFFER/THAT CAN BE ARRANGED** Tufton Arms Hotel has access to over 24 miles of the River Eden offering guests wild brown trout and salmon fishing on the lower reaches. There is also fishing on two tarns within the Pennines that are well stocked with rainbow trout. Brown trout fishing charged from £10 to £15 per rod per day. Salmon fishing charges vary from £15 to £60 per rod per day. Fly-fishing courses run by John Pape. Pheasant-, partridge- and grouse-shooting and duck flighting on local estates. The hotel also offers the complete season's shooting on the 2,500-acre Dalemain estate just north of Lake Ullswater. Golf and pony trekking locally.

**SEASONS/BEST TIMES FOR SPECIALIST SPORTS** Salmon: 15 January to 14 October; trout: 15 March to 30 September. Grouse: 12 August to 16 December; duck, pheasant and partridge from October.

**DOGS/CHILDREN WELCOME** Yes.

**ANY OTHER INFO** The Milsom family, which runs this renowned coaching house, is so keen on fieldsports that Nigel Milsom has set up a sporting agency within the hotel. Recommended by Egon Ronay and Johansens.

**HOW TO GET THERE** On A66 13 miles from Penrith. Junction 38 off the M6, 11 miles away.

Cavendish Hotel, Baslow, Derbyshire DE45 1SP
**Tel** 01246 582311 **Fax** 01246 582312
**e-mail** info@cavendish-hotel.net/ **website** www.cavendish-hotel.net
**Star ratings** ***AA Red

**NO OF ROOMS** 24.

**COST** From £95 per night for a single room only. From £125 per night for a standard double room only.

**SPECIAL BREAKS/OFFERS** Winter Weekends. Please enquire.

**FOOD** Restaurant, Garden Room and The Kitchen Table. The latter is a table for two in the kitchen where guests can see for themselves what takes place behind the scenes. Extensive and varied menu based on a modern British style. Cosmopolitan list of over 100 ready chilled or room-racked wines. The bar has a unique cocktail list, special whiskies and rare vintage ports. Awarded two AA rosettes and RAC Blue Ribbon.

**SPORT ON OFFER/THAT CAN BE ARRANGED** Brown trout and grayling fishing on the Rivers Derwent and Wye. Hunting with the High Peak Harriers and the Meynell Foxhounds.

**SEASONS/BEST TIMES FOR SPECIALIST SPORTS** Traditional seasons.

**DOGS/CHILDREN WELCOME** No dogs. Children welcome.

**ANY OTHER INFO** The Cavendish is set within the Chatsworth estate. All rooms overlook the estate and are furnished with antiques, works of art and original features such as open fires and oak beams. Originally this site belonged to The Peacock which belonged to the Duke of Rutland and served the turnpike between Chesterfield and Buxton. It became the Duke of Devonshire's in 1830 and was rebuilt as the Cavendish in the early Seventies. The hotel is famous as a gallery for proprietor Eric Marsh's eclectic collection of over 300 pictures which range from Victorian fine art to 20th-century graffiti. Gift shop.

**HOW TO GET THERE** M1 to junction 29. Take A619 to Baslow.

Riber Hall, Matlock, Derbyshire DE4 5JU
**Tel** 01629 582795 **Fax** 01629 580475
**e-mail** info@riber-hall.co.uk **website** www.riber-hall.co.uk
**Star ratings** ***AA

**NO OF ROOMS** 14.

**COST** From £95 per night bed and breakfast for a single room. From £123 per night bed and breakfast for a double room.

**SPECIAL BREAKS/OFFERS** Hideaway summer breaks: from £190 per person for two nights based on two people sharing including two dinners, two breakfasts and one afternoon tea. Hideaway winter breaks: from £180 per person as above.

**FOOD** English classical and French provincial. Extensive wine list with emphasis on New World wines. Awarded two AA rosettes.

**SPORT ON OFFER/THAT CAN BE ARRANGED** Trout fishing on the River Derwent and stocked local reservoirs. Clay pigeon shooting with British and Commonwealth chief coach Joe Neville, charged at £40 per 100 clays with tuition. Sailing on Carsington Water. Hunting with the High Peak Harriers, The Barlow and Meynell Foxhounds. Also riding, tennis and golf.

**SEASONS/BEST TIMES FOR SPECIALIST SPORTS** Traditional seasons.

**DOGS/CHILDREN WELCOME** Dogs welcome. Children over 10-years-old welcome.

**ANY OTHER INFO** This 15th-century manor house was established as a hotel by Alex Biggin in 1972. It stands within its own walled garden and orchard. Own outdoor tennis court. Johansens recommended.

**HOW TO GET THERE** Take M1 to junction 28. Take A 38 to Matlock for three miles and then A615 to Tansley. In Tansley turn into Alders Lane to the hotel.

The Lathkil Hotel, Over Haddon, Bakewell, Derbyshire DE45 1JE
**Tel** & **Fax** 01629 812501 **website** www.lathkil.co.uk

**NO OF ROOMS** Four.

**COST** From £37.50 per night bed and breakfast for single occupancy. From £55 to £70 per night bed and breakfast for a double room.

**SPECIAL BREAKS/OFFERS** Please enquire.

**FOOD** Home-cooked food both in the bar and on the restaurant's à la carte menu. Pizzas available in the evenings. Traditional beers, including Hartington Bitter. Select wine list.

**SPORT THAT CAN BE ARRANGED** Day tickets available on the River Wye for brown trout fishing. Otherwise arrangements can be made through Haddon Hall for fishing on the Rivers Wye, Lathkil and Bradford. Hunting with the High Peak Harriers. Also sailing, cycling and golf.

**SEASONS/BEST TIMES FOR SPECIALIST SPORTS** Traditional seasons.

**DOGS/CHILDREN** Dogs welcome in bedrooms charged at £5. Children welcome but there are no family rooms.

**ANY OTHER INFO** The Lathkil Hotel is situated above Lathkil Dale in the heart of the Peak National Park.

**HOW TO GET THERE** Take B5055 from Bakewell towards Monyash. After 1¼ miles turn left to Over Haddon and the hotel is a mile up the road.

The Wind In The Willows Hotel, Derbyshire Level, Glossop, Derbyshire SK13 9PT
**Tel** 01457 868001 **Fax** 01457 853354
**e-mail** info@windinthewillows.co.uk **website** www.windinthewillows.co.uk
**Star ratings** **AA

**NO OF ROOMS** 12.

**COST** From £72 per night bed and breakfast for a single room. From £99 per night bed and breakfast for a double/twin room.

**SPECIAL BREAKS/OFFERS** Summer four-day break: 25 per cent off the bed and breakfast rates. Winter two-day break: 33 per cent off the bed and breakfast rates.

**FOOD** Large varied menu with emphasis on home-cooking using fresh, local produce where possible. Selection of wines and malt whiskies. RAC Dining Award.

**SPORT ON OFFER/THAT CAN BE ARRANGED** Brown trout fishing on the River Derwent and on stocked lakes. Pheasant- and grouse-shooting on local estates and moors. Also riding, clay pigeon shooting and golf.

**SEASONS/BEST TIMES FOR SPECIALIST SPORTS** Traditional seasons.

**DOGS/CHILDREN WELCOME** No dogs. Children over 10-years old welcome.

**ANY OTHER INFO** The hotel is an early Victorian country house, set in five acres, which has retained its oak-panelled rooms, traditional furnishings and open fires. It is Kriss Akabusi's best hotel. "It's not particularly flamboyant, but the staff are nice and I feel at home there," he said. Johansens, Michelin, *Which? Hotel Guide*, *The Good Hotel Guide* recommended.

**HOW TO GET THERE** Take A57 out of Glossop. A mile later turn right opposite the Royal Oak pub. The hotel is 400yd on the right.

Combe House At Gittisham, Honiton, Near Exeter, Devon EX14 3AD
**Tel** 01404 540400 **Fax** 01404 46004
**e-mail** stay@thishotel.com **website** www.thishotel.com
**Star ratings** ***AA

**NO OF ROOMS** 15.

**COST** From £108 to £225 per night bed and breakfast for a double/twin room.

**SPECIAL BREAKS/OFFERS** Feast of Country: from £166 per night dinner, bed and breakfast for two people for a two-night break.

**FOOD** Contemporary British. Popular two-course Combe lunch £10 per person; three-course Sunday lunch £16.50 per person. Ancient underground cellars have been drained to provide optimum conditions for an extensive number of fine wines. Awarded two AA rosettes.

**SPORT ON OFFER/THAT CAN BE ARRANGED** Pheasant-shooting on the estate and also locally. Brown trout fishing on the hotel's own 1½mile stretch of the River Otter. Sea fishing at Beer and Lyme Regis. Hawk walks and falconry displays on the estate. Also golf and ballooning.

**SEASONS/BEST TIMES FOR SPECIALIST SPORTS** Traditional seasons.

**DOGS/CHILDREN WELCOME** Well behaved, yes. Dogs charges £5 a night. Children welcome.

**ANY OTHER INFO** Combe House is an Elizabethan manor set within its own 3,500-acre estate. It is run by Ruth and Ken Hunt who took over two years ago. The house is furnished with antiques, 18th-century family portraits, fresh flowers and carved oak panelling. Johansens recommended.

**HOW TO GET THERE** M5 travelling couth: junction 28 to Honiton, Heathpark and then Gittisham. A30/303. Come off at Honiton/Heathpark/Sidmouth/Cullompton and follow signs to Heathpark and Gittisham. M5/Exeter travelling north: junction 29 to the airport, then Honiton and turn off at Pattesons Cross for Fenny Bridges. Turn next right after Alfington/Ottery St Mary to Gittisham.

Half Moon Inn, Sheepwash, Near Hatherleigh, Devon EX12 5NE
**Tel** 01409 231376 **Fax** 01409 231673 **e-mail** nat@halfmoon.demon.co.uk
**Star ratings** Four crowns English Tourist Board

**NO OF ROOMS** 15. Three bedrooms on ground floor.

**COST** From £58.75 per person per night dinner, bed and breakfast.

**SPECIAL BREAKS/OFFERS** From £153 per person, dinner, bed and breakfast for a three-day break.

**FOOD** Renowned locally. All fresh and home cooked. Huge helpings. Bar snacks lunchtime, restaurant evenings. Very good value. Over 200 wines on offer. Benjie's Bar well known for the beer and range of malt whiskies.

**SPORT ON OFFER/THAT CAN BE ARRANGED** The hotel has private fishing on 10 miles of the River Torridge. Beats on the middle and lower Torridge are the river's best salmon and sea-trout waters. The Half Moon also has its own stillwater fishery with three lakes (six acres) stocking rainbow trout.

**SEASONS/BEST TIMES FOR SPECIALIST SPORTS** Salmon: mid-March to mid-May and September. Spinning allowed in March, thereafter fly only. Favourite flies: Yellow Torrisch, Silver Doctor, and Thunder & Lightening. Sea-trout up to 10lb enter the river late April and May. Main run starts in June with late June, July and August being the best times. Wet fly-fishing is the most-favoured method of fishing the Torridge. Favourite flies: Silver Butcher, Peter Ross, Mallard & Claret, Connemara Black, Silver Stoat's Tail. Brown trout: April, May and June. Favourite flies: Gold Ribbed Hare's Ear, Adam's, Black Gnat, Dark Olive, Coachman, Greenwell's Glory, Butcher and Pheasant Tail.

**DOGS/CHILDREN WELCOME** Yes.

**ANY OTHER INFO** Family-run hotel with exceptional atmosphere. Large rod room, drying facilities and tackle shop. Tuition and tackle available for hire. Licences issued at the inn.

**HOW TO GET THERE** A386 north from Okehampton. Turn right at Hatherleigh on to A3072. Four miles later turn right for Sheepwash.

Highbullen Hotel, Chittlehamholt, Umberleigh, Devon EX37 9HD
**Tel** 01769 540561 **Fax** 01769 540492
**e-mail** info@highbullen.co.uk **website** www.highbullen.co.uk
**Star ratings** ***AA

**NO OF ROOMS** 40.

**COST** From £60 to £90 per person per night dinner, bed and breakfast during the week. From £65 to £95 per person dinner, bed and breakfast staying Friday or Saturday night. This price includes unlimited golf on the hotel's own course.

**SPECIAL BREAKS/OFFERS** Seasonal breaks available from November to March. Please enquire.

**FOOD** English. Extensive wine list. Both restaurant and bar menus. Two dining-rooms.

**SPORT ON OFFER/THAT CAN BE ARRANGED** Salmon, sea- and brown trout fishing on five beats of the River Taw and its main tributary, the River Mole. All beats limited to two rods and each are about a mile long. Rods charged between £25 and £40 a day. Peter Keen, Julian Zealey and Roddy Rae are on hand to gillie and for tuition. Fishing can be arranged on the Rivers Lyn and Exe. Driven- and rough-shooting locally. Daily cruises to Lundy Island. Sailing from Ilfracombe or Bideford. Indoor and outdoor tennis. Golf on the hotel's own 18-hole course. Tuition available with resident professional, Paul Weston.

**SEASONS/BEST TIMES FOR SPECIALIST SPORTS** Salmon: 1 March to 30 September. Sea- and brown trout: 15 March to 30 September.

**DOGS/CHILDREN WELCOME** Dogs by prior arrangement. Children over eight-years-old welcome.

**ANY OTHER INFO** The Highbullen estate, owned by Hugh and Pam Neil since 1963, extends over 200 acres. The hotel is situated between the River Taw and Mole and is the only hotel on the Taw to own its own fishing. The house is a Victorian Gothic mansion designed and built by William Moore of Exeter. Also billiard room, sauna, steam room and sports shop.

**HOW TO GET THERE** M5 to Tiverton junction 27. Take A361 to South Molton and then B3226 to Crediton. Five miles later turn right to Chittlehamholt. The hotel is a mile beyond the village on the left.

Holne Chase Hotel, Near Ashburton, Devon TQ13 7NS
**Tel** 01364 631471 **Fax** 01364 631453
**e-mail** info@holne-chase.co.uk **website** www.holne-chase.co.uk
**Batty's e-mail** bark@batty-basset.co.uk **Batty's website** www.batty-basset.co.uk
**Star ratings** ***AA/English Tourist Board highly commended

**NO OF ROOMS** 17. Stable suites ideal for guests in need of room for sporting equipment and dog.

**COST** From £125 to £165 per night bed and breakfast for a double room.

**SPECIAL BREAKS/OFFERS** From £150 to £205 per night, dinner, bed and breakfast for a double room (minimum two-night stay). Benefits from membership of Holne Chase Club (HCC).

**FOOD** Traditional English with modern touches. Emphasis on local, seasonal produce. Three AA rosettes for food.

**SPORT ON OFFER/THAT CAN BE ARRANGED** Holne Chase owns a mile-long beat on the River Dart which is well known for its prolific run of sea-trout. There's fly-fishing on the hotel water or on Duchy water. Gillies and equipment hire available. Foxhunting with Dartmoor packs. Driven-, rough- and clay pigeon shooting arranged locally. Tennis, sailing, canoeing and golf locally.

**SEASONS/BEST TIMES FOR SPECIALIST SPORTS** Fly-fishing: April to end September. Fresh water fishing: February to December. Otherwise traditional seasons.

**DOGS/CHILDREN WELCOME** Dogs charged £5 a night. Children welcome, but no under 10-year-olds in the restaurant.

**ANY OTHER INFO** Holne Chase was a hunting lodge for the abbots at nearby Buckfast Abbey. Boots and walking sticks litter the porch and hosts Sebastian and Philippa Hughes' basset hogs the fire. A small charge for fishing the Dart has been introduced of which 25 per cent is donated for restocking and improvements. No charges for HCC members.

**HOW TO GET THERE** Take M5 south to Exeter then A38 towards Plymouth. Exit at the second Ashburton junction, and take road to Princetown/Dartmeet. Go over the River Dart at Holne Bridge and hotel is 200yd up on the right.

Lydford House Hotel, Lydford, Devon EX20 4AU
**Tel** 01822 820347 **Fax** 01822 820442 **e-mail** relax@lydfordhouse.co.uk
**Star ratings** **AA

**NO OF ROOMS** 12.

**COST** From £39.50 per person per night bed and breakfast in a single or double room.

**SPECIAL BREAKS/OFFERS** Spring/autumn/winter: from £99 per person dinner, bed and breakfast, a two-hour ride on Dartmoor. Based on two people sharing a double room.

**FOOD** Traditional using fresh, local, organic produce where possible. Over 30 bins on the wine list. Awarded RAC Dining Award.

**SPORT ON OFFER/THAT CAN BE ARRANGED** Riding across Dartmoor from the hotel's own stable of 25 horses and ponies. Hunting with Mid Devon and Spooners and West Dartmoor Foxhounds. Brown and rainbow trout fishing at local fisheries.

**SEASONS/BEST TIMES FOR SPECIALIST SPORTS** Spring/autumn for riding across Dartmoor.

**DOGS/CHILDREN WELCOME** Yes.

**ANY OTHER INFO** Andrew and Julie Searle have recently taken over Lydford House which was built for the local artist William Widgery in 1880. It is just a quarter of a mile from Dartmoor.

**HOW TO GET THERE** M5 to Exeter then A30. Turn off on to A386 to Tavistock. After four miles turn right into Lydford. Hotel is on the right.

Mill End Hotel, Sandy Park, Chagford, Devon TQ13 8JN
**Tel** 01647 432282 **Fax** 01647 433106 **e-mail** millendhotel@talk21.com
**Star ratings** ***AA

**NO OF ROOMS** 17.

**COST** From £32 to £55 per person bed and breakfast. From £55 to £80 per person dinner, bed and breakfast.

**SPECIAL BREAKS/OFFERS** Gourmet weekend in October and November. Also Spring Special and Christmas and New Year packages.

**FOOD** Modern British with classical French overtones. Desserts a speciality. Wine list offers 140 bins. Selection of cognacs and malt whiskies. Award winning cheese board. Awarded two AA rosettes.

**SPORT ON OFFER/THAT CAN BE ARRANGED** Salmon, sea-trout and brown trout fishing on the River Teign. Game-shooting locally. Hunting with the Mid Devon Foxhounds. Riding, pony trekking and golf.

**SEASONS/BEST TIMES FOR SPECIALIST SPORTS** Traditional seasons.

**DOGS/CHILDREN WELCOME** Very much so.

**ANY OTHER INFO** Mill End is a converted 18th-century watermill situated on the banks of the River Teign. It has a relaxed country-house atmosphere. It has been a hotel since 1929 and retains many of the original features. Ground-floor bedrooms have stone-flagged patios with tables and chairs adjoining lawns and garden.

**HOW TO GET THERE** Take M5 and A30 to Whiddon Down. Take A382 to Chagford and Moretonhampstead. The hotel is four miles from Whiddon Down on the right.

Prince Hall Hotel, Near Two Bridges, Dartmoor, Devon PL20 6SA
**Tel** 01822 890403 **Fax** 01822 890676
**e-mail** sporting@princehall.co.uk **website** www.princehall.co.uk
**Star ratings** **AA

**NO OF ROOMS** Nine.

**COST** From £72.50 per person per night dinner, bed and breakfast.

**SPECIAL BREAKS/OFFERS** Murder, Mystery Weekend from £160; Stillwater Fishing from £340; Gourmet Adventure from £160; Discovering Dartmoor from £160; Trout Fly-Fishing for Beginners from £345; and Trout Fly-Fishing for Improvers from £450. All prices are per person including dinner, bed and breakfast.

**FOOD** Menus are full of fresh local produce including Dartmoor venison and lamb, fish from Brixham, wild salmon and trout from the River Dart and herbs from the garden. There is also a comprehensive wine list of fine traditional and New World wines. Winner of the West Country Cooking award 2000. Awarded two AA rosettes.

**SPORT ON OFFER/THAT CAN BE ARRANGED** Fly-fishing on the River Dart. Foxhunting with Mid Devon, South Devon, Spooners and West Dartmoor and Dartmoor. Golf and hawking locally.

**SEASONS/BEST TIMES FOR SPECIALIST SPORTS** Fly-fishing from March to the end of September.

**DOGS/CHILDREN WELCOME** Well-behaved dogs are welcome free of charge. Hotel not suitable for children.

**ANY OTHER INFO** This hotel is set in the heart of Dartmoor. It exposes its guests to the beauty of the moor without idealising this primitive landscape. Prince Hall Hotel is a country house offering an 18th-century lifestyle in today's society through the hospitality of owner-managers Adam and Carrie Southwell.

**HOW TO GET THERE** From the M5: pass Exeter, take A38 to Plymouth. Come off at second Ashburton turn-off on to B3357 to Two Bridges and Princetown. Hotel is 10 miles farther on left. From Plymouth: take A386 to Yelverton. Follow signs for Princetown. Continue to Two Bridges, turn right and stay on B3357. Hotel is one mile farther on right.

The Arundell Arms, Lifton, Devon PL16 0AA
**Tel** 01566 784666 **Fax** 01566 784494 **e-mail** arundellarms@btinternet.com
**Star ratings** ***AA

**NO OF ROOMS** 28.

**COST** From £45 per person per night bed and breakfast.

**SPECIAL BREAKS/OFFERS** From £140 per person dinner, bed and breakfast for a two-night stay.

**FOOD** Restaurant presided over by master chefs Philip Burgess and Nick Shopland. Specialities include casserole of lobster, sole and scallops, South Devon beef and Cornish sea bass. Extensive wine list. Nominated Devon's Restaurant of the Year by T*he Good Food Guide*. Awarded three AA rosettes.

**SPORT ON OFFER/THAT CAN BE ARRANGED** Salmon, brown and sea-trout fishing on 20 private miles of the River Tamar and its tributaries. Brown and rainbow trout fishing on the hotel's own stocked three-acre lake. Gillies and tuition available. Fly-fishing school. Driven snipe-shooting. Also pheasant-, woodcock- and rough-shooting. Duck flighting locally. Hunting with Dartmoor foxhound packs. Pony trekking and golf.

**SEASONS/BEST TIMES FOR SPECIALIST SPORTS** Traditional seasons.

**DOGS/CHILDREN WELCOME** Yes.

**ANY OTHER INFO** The Arundell Arms is a former coaching inn on the Devon/Cornwall border, personally owned and run for 40 years by Anne Voss-Bark, herself a fisherman. She is married to Conrad Voss-Bark, former BBC parliamentary correspondent, and contributor to *The Times* on fly-fishing. Beginners fly-fishing courses for two to four days from £175 to £310 including all tackle. The 250-year-old former cock-fighting pit is now the hotel's rod and fishing tackle room.

**HOW TO GET THERE** Take M5 to Exeter, then A30 to Lifton. Hotel is half a mile off A30 in Lifton.

The Manor House Hotel And Golf Club, Moretonhampstead, Near Exeter,
Devon TQ13 8RE
**Tel** 01647 440355 **Fax** 01647 440961
**e-mail** reception.manorhouse@principalhotels.co.uk **website** www.principalhotels.co.uk
**Star ratings** ****AA

**NO OF ROOMS** 90.

**COST** From £59 dinner, bed and breakfast per person per night for a single or double room.

**SPECIAL BREAKS/OFFERS** Please enquire.

**FOOD** Traditional food offering best south west produce. Desserts a speciality. Broad selection of wines with emphasis on the New World. About 40 malt whiskies and 15 brandies on offer. Awarded an AA rosette.

**SPORT ON OFFER/THAT CAN BE ARRANGED** Brown trout fishing on seven miles of the Upper Teign, the River Bovey and the hotel's lake. Clay pigeon shooting. Own golf course which is home to the South West PGA Championships. Tennis. Hunting with the South Devon and Mid Devon Foxhounds. Hirelings available.

**SEASONS/BEST TIMES FOR SPECIALIST SPORTS** Traditional seasons.

**DOGS/CHILDREN WELCOME** Yes.

**ANY OTHER INFO** The Manor House is set within its own grounds on the edge of Dartmoor.

**HOW TO GET THERE** Take M5 to junction 31. Take A30. Turn off at Whiddon Down on to A382 to Moretonhampstead. Take B3213 to Princetown. The Manor House is on the left.

The Nobody Inn, Doddiscombsleigh, Near Exeter, Devon EX6 7PS
**Tel** 01647 252394 **Fax** 01647 252978
**e-mail** inn.nobody@virgin.net

**NO OF ROOMS** Seven.

**COST** From £23 per night bed and breakfast for a single room. From £55 per night bed and breakfast for a double room.

**SPECIAL BREAKS/OFFERS** Room rate is reduced by £2 per person for stays of four nights or more.

**FOOD** Bar and restaurant meals can be ordered from a small menu based on local produce. Well-stocked cellar offers 800 wines, as well as 250 whiskies, traditionally brewed beer, local cider, fine ports and brandies and home-made mulled wine. Restaurant open from Tuesday to Saturday. Specialist in Devon cheeses stocking over 30 varieties.

**SPORT THAT CAN BE ARRANGED** Brown trout fishing on the River Teign. Stocked rainbow trout fishing at Watercress Farm, Chudleigh, and Kennick Reservoir. Sea fishing at Teignmouth. Racing at Exeter.

**SEASONS/BEST TIMES FOR SPECIALIST SPORTS** Traditional seasons.

**DOGS/CHILDREN WELCOME** No dogs. Not suitable for children under 14-years-old.

**ANY OTHER INFO** According to legend, an unknown purchaser closed and locked the doors and refused hospitality to weary travellers. Upon receiving no answer to their knocking they continued on their journey in the belief there was nobody in – hence the pub's name. This 16th-century inn has long outlived its inhospitable past. Tutored wine tastings once a month. It also acts as a wine merchant. *Good Pub Guide* Wine Pub of the Year 1997, 1998 and 1999. Egon Ronay's Cheese Pub of the Year 1995.

**HOW TO GET THERE** Take the Dunchideock turning of A38 signed for Exeter racecourse. Follow signs for Doddiscombsleigh and The Nobody Inn is signposted from there.

The Rising Sun Hotel, Harbourside, Lynmouth, North Devon EX35 6EQ
**Tel** 01598 753223 **Fax** 01598 753480
**e-mail** risingsunlynmouth@easynet.co.uk **website** www.risingsunlynmouth.co.uk
**Star ratings** **AA

**NO OF ROOMS** 16.

**COST** From £47 per person per night bed and breakfast based on two people sharing a double room.

**SPECIAL BREAKS/OFFERS** From £74.50 per person per night dinner, bed and breakfast (minimum two-night stay).

**FOOD** Classic modern French and English cuisine. Local game and seafood specialities, especially lobster. Extensive wine list. Real ales. Awarded two AA rosettes.

**SPORT ON OFFER/THAT CAN BE ARRANGED** Salmon, sea-trout and brown trout fishing on the hotel's own stretch of the East Lyn River. Sea fishing. Pheasant-shooting at Lillycombe and other local estates. Hunting with the Devon & Somerset Staghounds and the Exmoor Foxhounds. Golf.

**SEASONS/BEST TIMES FOR SPECIALIST SPORTS** Traditional seasons.

**DOGS/CHILDREN WELCOME** Sadly, no.

**ANY OTHER INFO** The Rising Sun, a historic thatched 14th-century smugglers' inn, overlooks a tiny harbour and the East Lyn River. It is owned by Hugo and Pamela Jeune. Mr Jeune, a Liveryman of the Worshipful Company of Distillers, is a keen shot when time allows. Bedrooms furnished by Suzanne Lansdell. Oak-panelled dining-room and bar, crooked ceilings and uneven oak floors. Recommended by Egon Ronay, Johansens and *Which? Hotel Guide*.

**HOW TO GET THERE** M5 junction 23. A39 to Minehead and then to Lynmouth. Hotel at harbour side.

The Staghunters Hotel, Brendon, Lynton, North Devon EX35 6PS
**Tel** 01598 741222 **Fax** 01598 741352 **e-mail** staghunters@netscapeonline.co.uk
**Star ratings** Three Crowns commended

**NO OF ROOMS** 12.

**COST** From £30 per person per night bed and breakfast.

**SPECIAL BREAKS/OFFERS** From £85 per person bed and breakfast (minimum two-night stay) or £120 per person bed and breakfast for a three-night stay.

**FOOD** Food made from local produce. Both bar and restaurant meals. Well-stocked cellar and good choice of beer including local Exmoor Real Ale.

**SPORT THAT CAN BE ARRANGED** Salmon and both sea-trout and brown trout fishing on East Lyn. Pheasant-shooting at Lillycombe. Hunting with Exmoor Foxhounds and Devon & Somerset Staghounds. Stabling available. Golf nearby.

**SEASONS/BEST TIMES FOR SPECIALIST SPORTS** Traditional seasons.

**DOGS/CHILDREN WELCOME** Yes.

**ANY OTHER INFO** This small family-run hotel rests on the banks of the River Lyn in the heart of the Doone Valley, famously bought to life by R D Blackmore. The Exmoor Foxhounds not only meet at the hotel once a year, they also holds their hunt ball here.

**HOW TO GET THERE** Just off A39 between Lynmouth and Porlock.

Plumber Manor, Sturminster Newton, Dorset DT10 2AF
**Tel** 01258 472507 **Fax** 01258 473370
**e-mail** book@plumbermanor.com
**Star ratings** ***AA

**NO OF ROOMS** 16.

**COST** From £80 per night bed and breakfast for a single room. From £47.50 to £72.50 per person per night in a double room based on two people sharing.

**SPECIAL BREAKS/OFFERS** Minimum two-night stays from March to November. Please enquire.

**FOOD** English and French cuisine using local fresh produce prepared by Brian Prideaux-Brune. Extensive wine list. The main bar and dining-rooms have open fires. The restaurant is divided into three rooms. Awarded two AA rosettes.

**SPORT ON OFFER/THAT CAN BE ARRANGED** Hunting with the Portman and Blackmore & Sparkford Vale Foxhounds. Coarse fishing on the River Stour. Clay pigeon shooting and golf.

**SEASONS/BEST TIMES FOR SPECIALIST SPORTS** Traditional seasons.

**DOGS/CHILDREN WELCOME** By prior arrangement.

**ANY OTHER INFO** Plumber was built in the early 17th century by Charles Brune and has since remained a family home for the Prideaux-Brunes. The Divelish stream, a tributary of the River Stour, runs through the grounds. Ten further bedrooms are available in the courtyard. The hotel is closed in February.

**HOW TO GET THERE** From Sturminster Newton take the Sherborne road. After half a mile turn left for Hazelbury Bryan. The hotel is two miles down the road.

The Anvil Hotel, Salisbury Road, Pimperne, Blandford, Dorset DT11 8UQ
**Tel** 01258 453431 **Fax** 01258 480182
**Star ratings** ***English Tourist Board

**NO OF ROOMS** 11.

**COST** From £50 per night bed and breakfast for a single room. From £75 per night bed and breakfast for a double room.

**SPECIAL BREAKS/OFFERS** Mini break: from £120 for two people bed and breakfast (minimum two-night stay).

**FOOD** Both à la carte restaurant and bar menus. Emphasis on fresh local produce down to the butter served. Venison a speciality. Comprehensive wine list.

**SPORT ON OFFER/THAT CAN BE ARRANGED** Coarse fishing on the River Stour. Stocked brown and rainbow trout fishing locally. Pheasant- and partridge-shooting on farms and estates within a 20-mile radius. Roe deer stalking with owner Colin Palmer on 6,000 acres of local estates. Clay pigeon shooting.

**SEASONS/BEST TIMES FOR SPECIALIST SPORTS** Traditional seasons.

**DOGS/CHILDREN WELCOME** Yes.

**ANY OTHER INFO** The Anvil, a 16th-century thatched inn owned and run by Carolann and Colin Palmer, is set in a typical English garden. The manor house was given by Henry VIII to Catherine Howard and on her death, to Catherine Parr.

**HOW TO GET THERE** On A354 Salisbury road.

The Half Moon, Half Moon Street, Sherborne, Dorset DT9 3LN
**Tel** 01935 812017 **Fax** 01936 815295 **website** www.lionheartinns.demon.co.uk
**Star ratings** Five AA diamonds/Les Routiers Silver Key

**NO OF ROOMS** 16.

**COST** From £54 per night bed and breakfast for a single room. From £69 per night bed and breakfast for a double room.

**SPECIAL BREAKS/OFFERS** Please enquire.

**FOOD** Full à la carte and bar menu. Carvery a speciality. Extensive wine list.

**SPORT THAT CAN BE ARRANGED** Pheasant-shooting on local estates and farms. Clay pigeon shooting. Hunting with the Blackmore & Sparkford Vale Foxhounds. Brown trout fishing on local rivers. Fishing on lakes in Sherborne Castle. Also sea fishing and golf.

**SEASONS/BEST TIMES FOR SPECIALIST SPORTS** Traditional seasons.

**DOGS/CHILDREN WELCOME** No dogs. Children welcome.

**ANY OTHER INFO** The Half Moon has been a pub since the 16th century although it was bombed during the war. Very popular with the locals.

**HOW TO GET THERE** From London and the South: A30 then A352 to Sherborne. From the North: M5 junction 29 then A303 then A352 to Sherborne.

Bibury Court Hotel, Bibury, Near Cirencester, Gloucestershire GL7 5NT
**Tel** 01285 740337 **Fax** 01285 740660
**e-mail** reservations@biburycourt.co.uk **website** biburycourt.co.uk
**Star ratings** ***AA

**NO OF ROOMS** 18.

**COST** From £75 per night bed and Continental breakfast for a single room. From £105 per night bed and Continental breakfast for a double room. From £150 per night bed and Continental breakfast for a suite.

**SPECIAL BREAKS/OFFERS** From £150 per person on a two-night break to include dinner, Continental breakfast and accommodation. From £155 per room on a one-night break to include dinner, Continental breakfast and accommodation.

**FOOD** Traditional English cuisine with a Mediterranean influence. Fresh local produce used where possible. Bibury trout popular choice. Extensive wine list of 70 bins. Awarded two AA rosettes.

**SPORT ON OFFER/THAT CAN BE ARRANGED** Hunting with the Heythrop and Vale of White Horse Foxhounds. Game-shooting locally. Wild brown trout fishing on the hotel's own stretch of the River Coln. Also golf and riding.

**SEASONS/BEST TIMES FOR SPECIALIST SPORTS** Traditional seasons.

**DOGS/CHILDREN WELCOME** Dogs charged £3 per night. Children £35 per night.

**ANY OTHER INFO** Bibury Court dates from Tudor times although the main part was built by Sir Thomas Sackville in 1633. The interior was remodelled in 1759 and again in 1922. Sir Thomas, an illegitimate son of the first Earl of Dorset, was a "Knight and gentleman-usher in dailie waiting on the King James I". Charles II is reputed to have visited when he attended Bibury races, as did the Prince Regent during the reign of George III. The house remained in the Sackville family for several generations and through the female line passed through the Cresswells who sold the house, owing to a disputed will and years of litigation, to Lord Sherborne. Charles Dickens is said to have written Bleak House with this court case in mind. It was turned into a hotel in 1968 and is now owned by Jane Collier and Andrew and Anne Johnston.

**HOW TO GET THERE** From Cirencester: take B4425 through Barnsley. In Bibury bear right over the bridge along the river front. Turn right as the road bears left into the hotel. From A40 (Oxford): B4425 through Aldsworth. Down the steep hill into Bibury and turn left into the hotel.

Calcot Manor Hotel, Near Tetbury, Gloucestershire GL8 8YJ
**Tel** 01666 890391 **Fax** 01666 890394
**e-mail** reception@calcotmanor.co.uk **website** www.calcotmanor.co.uk
**Star ratings** ***AA Red

**NO OF ROOMS** 28.

**COST** From £110 per night bed and breakfast for a single room. From £145 to £170 per night bed and breakfast for a double/twin room.

**SPECIAL BREAKS/OFFERS** From £195 per night bed and breakfast in a deluxe room, £25 per person allowance towards dinner, minimum two-night stay from Sunday to Thursday.

**FOOD** Gumstool Inn (bistro) and The Conservatory Restaurant. Menus follow the seasons with fresh local produce sitting alongside delicate exotica on the extensive and varied menus. Draught beer on offer in the bar. Extensive wine list. Awarded two AA rosettes.

**SPORT ON OFFER/THAT CAN BE ARRANGED** Hunting with the Beaufort. Clay pigeon shooting. Also watersports, golf, swimming, croquet, tennis and cycling (hotel's own bikes).

**SEASONS/BEST TIMES FOR SPECIALIST SPORTS** Traditional seasons.

**DOGS/CHILDREN WELCOME** No dogs. Children welcome.

**ANY OTHER INFO** Calcot Manor Hotel is a handsome Cotswold farmhouse. Cistercian monks used to farm Calcot and the 14th-century tithe barn remains within the grounds. Flagstones lead to the arched front door made of old English oak. The hotel is owned by Michael and Louisa Stone. Their daughter, Nicki Farquhar, designed the interior. The immaculate gardens are surrounded by dry stone walls. Outdoor swimming pool. Tennis court.

**HOW TO GET THERE** Calcot Manor is three miles west of Tetbury, 12 miles from M4 junctions 17 and 18.

Corse Lawn House Hotel, Corse Lawn, Gloucester, Gloucestershire GL19 4LZ
**Tel** 01452 780771 **Fax** 01452 780840
**e-mail** hotel@corselawnhouse.u-net.com **website** www.corselawnhousehotel.co.uk
**Star ratings** ***AA

**NO OF ROOMS** 19.

**COST** From £75 per night bed and breakfast for a single room. From £120 per night bed and breakfast for a double room.

**SPECIAL BREAKS/OFFERS** From £155 per night dinner, bed and breakfast for a double room; from £140 for more than one night.

**FOOD** Table d'hôte and à la carte menus available most evenings. Restaurant in *The Good Food Guide* for 22 years. Also Egon Ronay, Michelin and AA recommended. Renowned wine cellar with over 400 wines.

**SPORT ON OFFER/THAT CAN BE ARRANGED** Pheasant- and partridge-shooting on local estates. Hunting with Ledbury Foxhounds. Well situated for Cheltenham racecourse. Heated indoor swimming pool. Tennis courts and golf nearby.

**SEASONS/BEST TIMES FOR SPECIALIST SPORTS** November to February.

**DOGS/CHILDREN WELCOME** Yes.

**ANY OTHER INFO** Corse Lawn is an elegant Queen Anne Grade II-listed building set in its own 12 acres. The house has belonged to the Hine family (of Cognac fame) since 1978. The hotel hosts the opening meet of the Ledbury Foxhounds.

**HOW TO GET THERE** From Birmingham: M5 to junction 8 (M50). Get off M50 and take A38 to Tewkesbury. Three miles later turn right on to A438 towards Ledbury. Go three miles and turn left on to B4211. Follow signs to Corse Lawn.
From Wales: M50 to junction 2. Take A417 to Gloucester. After Staunton turn left on to B4211. Follow signs to Corse Lawn.
From South: M5 to junction 12. Follow signs to Gloucester, then the Docks and then Ross-on-Wye. The other side of Gloucester take A417 to Ledbury. Six miles later turn right on to the B4211. Follow signs to Corse Lawn.
From London: M4 to junction 15. Take A419 towards Cirencester then follow A417 to Gloucester. Follow signs to Ledbury and Ross-on-Wye. Take A417 to Ledbury. Six miles later turn right on to B4211. Follow signs to Corse Lawn.

Fosse Manor Hotel, Stow-on-the-Wold, Cheltenham, Gloucestershire GL54 1UX
**Tel** 01451 830354 **Fax** 01451 832486 **e-mail** fossemanor@bestwestern.co.uk
**Star ratings** ***AA

**NO OF ROOMS** 23.

**COST** From £98 to £160 per night bed and breakfast for a double room.

**SPECIAL BREAKS/OFFERS** From £68 to £78 per person per night dinner, bed and breakfast based on two people sharing a double room.

**FOOD** Traditional English and Continental. Both table d'hôte and à la carte menus in restaurant. Bar meals. Grill stones a speciality. About 30 wines on offer.

**SPORT ON OFFER/THAT CAN BE ARRANGED** Pheasant-shooting locally. Hunting with the Heythrop Foxhounds. Trout fishing at Stanlake. Also archery, golf, quad bikes and clay pigeon shooting. Racing locally.

**SEASONS/BEST TIMES FOR SPECIALIST SPORTS** Traditional seasons.

**DOGS/CHILDREN WELCOME** Yes.

**ANY OTHER INFO** Bob and Yvonne Johnson bought Fosse Manor 30 years ago. Bob Johnson was a very successful carriage driver and is now a well respected judge. Hotel is very popular during the Cheltenham Festival.

**HOW TO GET THERE** A mile south of Stow-on-the-Wold on A429 Old Fosse Way.

Hatton Court Hotel, Upton Hill, Upton-St-Leonards, Gloucestershire GL4 8DE
**Tel** 01452 617412 **Fax** 01452 612945
**e-mail** res@hatton-court-co.uk **website** www.hatton-hotels.co.uk
**Star ratings** ***AA

**NO OF ROOMS** 45.

**COST** From £99 to £145 bed and breakfast per night for a double room.

**SPECIAL BREAKS/OFFER** From £99.50 dinner, bed and breakfast per night for a double room.

**FOOD** Traditional English. Fresh local produce used where possible. Daily chef specials. Member of the Glorious Gloucestershire Food Group which promotes local produce and businesses. The restaurant, Carrington's, is renowned locally. Extensive wine list with 200 bins housed in the restaurant's wine shop. The restaurant used to have two rosettes and aims to re-achieve that status with the new chef.

**SPORT ON OFFER/THAT CAN BE ARRANGED** Laser clay pigeon shooting. Also archery, crossbow- and air-rifle shooting. Local river and lake fishing.

**SEASONS/BEST TIMES FOR SPECIALIST SPORTS** Traditional seasons.

**DOGS/CHILDREN WELCOME** No dogs. Children welcome.

**ANY OTHER INFO** Hatton Court is a typical 17th-century Cotswold manor house. A Mr Hiscox, better known as ARH, was a Wiltshire lad who started off with a milk round and by the Seventies had a transport fleet and was a self-made multi-millionaire. He bought the hotel for he and his friends to meet in and enjoy a good meal. The hotel is now owned by Darren Hiscox. Extensive grounds. Also sauna, gym and jacuzzi. Civil wedding licence.

**HOW TO GET THERE** Leave Gloucester centre on B4073 towards Painswick. Continue up the hill and the hotel is on the right.

The Frogmill Inn, Andoversford, Cheltenham, Gloucestershire GL54 4HT
**Tel** 01242 820547 **Fax** 01242 820237
**website** www.frogmill.co.uk

**NO OF ROOMS** 16.

**COST** From £45 per night bed and breakfast for a single room. From £60 per night bed and breakfast for a double room.

**SPECIAL BREAKS/OFFERS** Stay Friday and Saturday night, get Sunday free.

**FOOD** Traditional English cooking.

**SPORT ON OFFER/THAT CAN BE ARRANGED** Hunting with the Cotswold and Heythrop Foxhounds. Rifle-shooting locally. Also golf and trial biking.

**SEASONS/BEST TIMES FOR SPECIALIST SPORTS** Traditional seasons.

**DOGS/CHILDREN WELCOME** Yes.

**ANY OTHER INFO** The Frogmill is mentioned in the Domesday Book as a working mill in 1087. It was converted into a coaching inn during the 1600s and retains features from that period such as open fires, wooden beams and stone walls. The hotel is set within five acres and the River Coln runs through the grounds. Very popular during the Cheltenham Festival.

**HOW TO GET THERE** Six miles east of Cheltenham on A40 turn right on to A436 after the Andoversford turning.

The Greenway Hotel, Shurdington, Cheltenham, Gloucestershire GL51 5UG
**Tel** 01242 862352 **Fax** 01242 862780 **e-mail** greenway@btconnect.com
**Star ratings** ***AA Red

**NO OF ROOMS** 19. Four ground-floor bedrooms.

**COST** From £79 per person dinner, bed and breakfast in a double room, based on two people sharing (minimum two-night stay).

**SPECIAL BREAKS/OFFERS** Please enquire.

**FOOD** Menu produced in a modern English way with a Mediterranean twist. It is based on fresh local produce, with an emphasis on local venison, fish and risottos. Conservatory dining-room. Extensive wine cellar holding 200 bins. Awarded three AA rosettes.

**SPORT ON OFFER/THAT CAN BE ARRANGED** Pheasant-shooting on the Brimpsfield and Coombe End estates. Clay pigeon shooting. Also golf, tennis, swimming and flying.

**SEASONS/BEST TIMES FOR SPECIALIST SPORTS** Traditional seasons.

**DOGS/CHILDREN WELCOME** No.

**ANY OTHER INFO** The Greenway was originally a manor house dating from the 16th century. It takes its name from the pre-Roman park which runs beside the hotel to Long Barrow, an early burial site. It is surrounded by 10 acres of grounds and gardens. Furnished with antiques and open fires.

**HOW TO GET THERE** The hotel is off A46 Cheltenham to Stroud road.

The Malt House, Broad Campden, near Chipping Campden, Gloucestershire GL55 6UU
**Tel** 01386 840295 **Fax** 01386 841334
**e-mail** nick@the-malt-house.freeserve.co.uk **website** www.malt-house.co.uk
**Star ratings** Five AA diamonds/Red House Michelin

**NO OF ROOMS** Eight.

**COST** From £69.50 (low season) to £117.50 (high season) per night bed and breakfast for a double room.

**SPECIAL BREAKS/OFFERS** Winter breaks. Please enquire.

**FOOD** Modern British. Fresh local produce used. Fruit, vegetables and herbs sourced from hotel's own garden. Extensive wine list. Awarded two AA rosettes.

**SPORT THAT CAN BE ARRANGED** Hunting with the North Cotswold and Heythrop Foxhounds. Clay pigeon shooting. Trout fishing at Donnington Fishery. For river fishing please enquire. Also golf and cycling.

**SEASONS/BEST TIMES FOR SPECIALIST SPORTS** Traditional seasons.

**DOGS/CHILDREN WELCOME** Yes.

**ANY OTHER INFO** The Malt House is owned and run by Nick Brown. There has been a building on the site since the 1530s and is known to be where monks brewed a heavy grain beer. The Earl of Gainsborough bought the house for his second son. Large garden.

**HOW TO GET THERE** A44 then B4081 to Chipping Campden. Follow signs for Broad Campden and the Malt House is in the centre of the village.

The Prestbury House Hotel And Restaurant, The Burgage, Prestbury, Cheltenham, Gloucestershire GL52 3DN
**Tel** 01242 529533 **Fax** 01242 227076
**website** www.smoothhound.co.uk
**Star ratings** ***AA/****English Tourist Board

**NO OF ROOMS** 17.

**COST** From £66 per night bed and breakfast for a single room. From £80 per night bed and breakfast for a double/twin.

**SPECIAL BREAKS AND OFFERS** From £130 for two nights, bed and breakfast based on two sharing a double room.

**FOOD** Traditional English and French cuisine popular with local clientele. Three restaurants serving both à la carte and table d'hôte menus. Michelin and RAC dining awards. Bar snacks available. Extensive wine cellar includes some distinctive dessert wines.

**SPORT THAT CAN BE ARRANGED** Helicopter ride to nearby estate for pheasant- and rough-shooting. Also racing.

**SEASONS/BEST TIMES FOR SPECIALIST SPORTS** Traditional seasons.

**DOGS/CHILDREN WELCOME** No dogs. Children welcome.

**ANY OTHER INFO** Prestbury House Hotel faces Cheltenham racecourse so is ideally situated for the National Hunt Festival. The 300-year-old typical William and Mary country manor sits within its own five acres of grounds, and yet is close to Cheltenham town centre. The coach house and stables hold further accommodation. Prestbury is reputed to be the most haunted village in England and so it is not surprising that the hotel grounds are noted for their spiritual sightings.

**HOW TO GET THERE** Follow signs to Cheltenham racecourse. The hotel is signposted from there.

Three Ways House, Mickleton, Chipping Campden, Gloucestershire GL55 6SB
**Tel** 01386 438429 **Fax** 01386 438118
**Star ratings** ***AA

**NO OF ROOMS** 41.

**COST** From £95 to £120 per night bed and breakfast for a double room.

**SPECIAL BREAKS/OFFERS** Minimum two-night stay from £65 per person per night dinner, bed and breakfast.

**FOOD** Fine food from fresh local produce where possible. Puddings a speciality. Extensive wine list featuring New World wines. Awarded an AA rosette.

**SPORT ON OFFER/THAT CAN BE ARRANGED** Hunting with the North Cotswold and Heythrop Foxhounds. Pheasant- and partridge-shooting on local estates. Clay pigeon shooting. Trout and carp fishing at Leamington Lake. Coarse fishing on the River Avon.

**SEASONS/BEST TIMES FOR SPECIALIST SPORTS** Traditional seasons.

**DOGS/CHILDREN WELCOME** Yes.

**ANY OTHER INFO** Privately owned and managed by Peter Henderson and Simon Coombe. This hotel is home to the Pudding Club which was set up to "prevent the demise of the Great British Pudding" and goes from strength to strength. Membership throughout the UK.

**HOW TO GET THERE** On B4632 in the middle of the village.

The Wild Duck Inn, Drakes Island, Ewen, Cirencester, Gloucestershire GL7 6BY
**Tel** 01285 770310 **Fax** 01285 770924 **e-mail** wduckinn@aol.com
**Star ratings** ***AA

**NO OF ROOMS** 11.

**COST** From £55 per night bed and breakfast for a single room. From£75 per night bed and breakfast for a standard double room.

**SPECIAL BREAKS/OFFERS** From June to September the second night is half price if the first night is a Saturday.

**FOOD** Traditional and homemade with emphasis on game and fish in season. Extensive wine list. Traditional beers. Awarded an AA rosette.

**SPORT ON OFFER/THAT CAN BE ARRANGED** Watersports and polo. Hunting with the Vale of White Horse, Beaufort and Heythrop Foxhounds. Pheasant- and partridge-shooting on local estates. Golf locally.

**SEASONS/BEST TIMES FOR SPECIALIST SPORTS** Traditional seasons.

**DOGS/CHILDREN WELCOME** Dogs by prior arrangement. Children welcome.

**ANY OTHER INFO** Traditional country pub with a feel for fine wine and food. Popular with locals and sporting enthusiasts.

**HOW TO GET THERE** Turn off A429 from or to Cirencester and follow signs to Ewen.

Ashburn Hotel And Restaurant, Station Road, Fordingbridge, Hampshire SP6 1JP
**Tel** 01425 652060 **Fax** 01425 652150 **e-mail** ashburn@mistral.co.uk
**Star ratings** **AA/English Tourist Council Silver award

**NO OF ROOMS** 20.

**COST** From £39.50 per night bed and breakfast for a single room. From £74 per night bed and breakfast for double/twin room.

**SPECIAL BREAKS/OFFERS** From £80 per person dinner, bed and breakfast (minimum two-night stay). From £114 per person dinner, bed and breakfast (minimum three-night stay).

**FOOD** Both table d'hôte and à la carte menus offering French/English cuisine. Vegetarian meals available. Wine list offers about 32 wines focusing mainly on New World and French varieties. Awarded an AA rosette and RAC dining award.

**SPORT ON OFFER/THAT CAN BE ARRANGED** Coarse fishing on the River Avon and local lakes. Fly-fishing at Rockbourne Trout Fisheries. Also riding, watersports, cycling, swimming and golf.

**SEASONS/BEST TIMES FOR SPECIALIST SPORTS** Traditional seasons.

**DOGS/CHILDREN WELCOME** Yes.

**ANY OTHER INFO** The Ashburn Hotel, owned and run by Garry and Terri Robson, is set within an acre of landscaped gardens which run down to the River Avon. Outdoor swimming pool.

**HOW TO GET THERE** Take M27 (west) to junction 1. Take B3079 to Fordingbridge. Left at the mini roundabout, right at fork to Sandheath and Damerham and follow for half a mile to the hotel.

Esseborne Manor Hotel, Hurstbourne Tarrant, Andover, Hampshire SP11 0ER
**Tel** 01264 736444 **Fax** 01264 736725 **e-mail** esseborne_manor@compuserve.com
**Star ratings** ***AA

**NO OF ROOMS** 14. Ground-floor rooms suitable for disabled guests.

**COST** From £100 to £160 per night bed and breakfast for a double room.

**SPECIAL BREAKS/OFFERS** From £300 for two nights' dinner, bed and breakfast for two people.

**FOOD** English cooking using local produce and herbs from the hotel's own herb garden. Game a speciality in season. During the summer guests may dine on the lawn. Extensive wine list. Selection of malt whiskies. Awarded two AA rosettes.

**SPORT ON OFFER/THAT CAN BE ARRANGED** Wild brown trout fishing on the River Test. Pheasant- and partridge-shooting on local estates. Also golf, croquet, tennis and race car driving.

**SEASONS/BEST TIMES FOR SPECIALIST SPORTS** Traditional seasons.

**DOGS/CHILDREN WELCOME** Dogs welcome but not in the main hotel. Children welcome but not in the restaurant in the evenings.

**ANY OTHER INFO** Esseborne Manor is set within three acres of landscaped gardens and owned and run by Ian Hamilton. Own tennis court. Civil wedding licence.

**HOW TO GET THERE** Midway between Andover and Newbury on A343.

Lainston House Hotel, Sparsholt, Winchester, Hampshire SO21 2LT
**Tel** 01962 863588 **Fax** 01962 776672
**e-mail** enquiries@lainstonhouse.com **website** www.exclusivehotels.co.uk
**Star ratings** ****AA

**NO OF ROOMS** 41.

**COST** From £95 per night for a single room (room only). From £145 per night for a double room (room only).

**SPECIAL BREAKS/OFFERS** From £110 per person per night dinner, bed and breakfast for a double room based on two people sharing (minimum two-night stay) – known as a Weekend Summer Break.

**FOOD** Gourmet English cooking with good European influences using local produce. Usually à la carte menu but on Friday and Saturday evenings a five-course candlelight menu is available. Also Lawn menu for alfresco dining during the summer. Extensive selection of wines and cognacs. Awarded two AA rosettes.

**SPORT ON OFFER/THAT CAN BE ARRANGED** Brown trout fishing on the River Test from £140 plus VAT per rod per day. Also gillie available for tuition and/or guide. Game-shooting on nearby estates. Clay pigeon shooting, tennis and croquet. Gym on site.

**SEASONS/BEST TIMES FOR SPECIALIST SPORTS** Fishing: every Friday from 14 April to 13 October.

**DOGS/CHILDREN WELCOME** Yes.

**ANY OTHER INFO** Lainston House is a 17th-century William and Mary country house surrounded by 63 acres of parkland in which are many rare shrubs and trees contributing to the renowned gardens. A spectacular avenue of lime trees is visible from the restaurant.

**HOW TO GET THERE** Lainston House is well signposted off B3049 Winchester to Stockbridge road, 2½ miles from Winchester.

The Chewton Glen Hotel, Christchurch Road, New Milton, Hampshire BH25 6QS
**Tel** 01425 275341 **Fax** 01425 272310
**e-mail** reservations@chewtonglen.com **website** www.chewtonglen.com
**Star ratings** *****AA Red/RAC Gold Ribbon

**NO OF ROOMS** 55.

**COST** From £235 per night for a double room only. From £365 per night dinner, bed and breakfast for a double room based on two people sharing.

**SPECIAL BREAKS/OFFERS** Please enquire.

**FOOD** Classic French/modern English cuisine with a healthier, lighter modern style. Extensive wine list. One Michelin star.

**SPORT ON OFFER/THAT CAN BE ARRANGED** Fishing and shooting can be arranged locally. Also sailing, two indoor and two outdoor tennis courts. Indoor and outdoor swimming pools. Own nine-hole golf course. Health club and spa. Riding locally.

**SEASONS/BEST TIMES FOR SPECIALIST SPORTS** Traditional seasons.

**DOGS/CHILDREN WELCOME** No dogs. Kennels available locally. Children welcome over six-years-old.

**ANY OTHER INFO** Chewton Glen is a privately owned, luxury country house hotel set on the edge of the New Forest and close to the sea. Voted Best Country House Hotel by *Gourmet* magazine.

**HOW TO GET THERE** A35 from Lyndhurst. Travel 10 miles and then turn left at the staggered junction following brown signs to the hotel and signed to Walkford.

The Master Builder's House Hotel, Buckler's Hard, Beaulieu, Hampshire SO42 7XB
**Tel** 01590 616253 **Fax** 01590 616297 **e-mail** res@themasterbuilders.co.uk
**Star ratings** ***AA

**NO OF ROOMS** 25.

**COST** From £110 per night bed and breakfast for a single room. From £145 to £195 per night bed and breakfast for a double room.

**SPECIAL BREAKS/OFFERS** From £175 per night dinner, bed and breakfast for a double room (minimum two-night stay).

**FOOD** Both à la carte and bar menus. Fresh local produce used where possible. Extensive wine list. Awarded two AA rosettes.

**SPORT ON OFFER/THAT CAN BE ARRANGED** Pheasant-shooting and brown trout fishing on the Beaulieu estate. Also sailing, watersports and golf.

**SEASONS/BEST TIMES FOR SPECIALIST SPORTS** Traditional seasons.

**DOGS/CHILDREN WELCOME** Dogs by prior arrangement. Children welcome.

**ANY OTHER INFO** Buckler's Hard was a well-known ship builders' yard and the hotel was the master builder Henry Adams' house. It is right on the edge of the Solent and an ideal setting for those keen on sailing. The hotel has been owned by Jeremy Wilcock and John Illsley since 1997.

**HOW TO GET THERE** M3, M27 west to the Fawley junction. Take A326 and then B3054 to Beaulieu and follow signs to Buckler's Hard.

Upland Park Hotel, Garrison Hill, Droxford, Southampton, Hampshire SO32 3QL
**Tel** 01489 878507 **Fax** 01489 877853 **e-mail** clarelay@globalnet.co.uk
**Star ratings** **AA

**NO OF ROOMS** 17.

**COST** From £40 per night bed and breakfast for a single room. From £56 per night bed and breakfast in a double room.

**SPECIAL BREAKS/OFFERS** Summer Madness: from £90 dinner, bed and breakfast (£30 supper) for two people.

**FOOD** Both table d'hôte and à la carte menus. Recommended by Les Routiers.

**SPORT ON OFFER/THAT CAN BE ARRANGED** Trout fishing on the hotel's own lake. Golf, swimming and sailing.

**SEASONS/BEST TIMES FOR SPECIALIST SPORTS** Traditional seasons.

**DOGS/CHILDREN WELCOME** Yes.

**ANY OTHER INFO** Upland Park is set within 10 acres in the heart of the Meon valley. Own outdoor swimming pool.

**HOW TO GET THERE** M27 to junction 10. A32 to Alton. Or, from A3/M3 take A272 and then A32 south.

Wykeham Arms, 75 Kingsgate Street, Winchester, Hampshire SO23 9PE
**Tel** 01962 853834 **Fax** 01962 854411

**NO OF ROOMS** 14.

**COST** From £45 to £99 per night bed and breakfast for a single room. From £79.50 to £117.50 per night bed and breakfast for a double/twin room.

**FOOD** Traditional food with Mediterranean influences. Varied menu with emphasis on local products. Hampshire Down lamb a speciality. Real ales and an extensive wine list closely associated with the wine shop also owned by Graeme Jameson. Twenty wines available by the glass. Four bars with open fires.

**SPORT ON OFFER/THAT CAN BE ARRANGED** Fishing on the Test and Itchen. Golf.

**SEASONS/BEST TIMES FOR SPECIALIST SPORTS** Traditional seasons.

**DOGS/CHILDREN WELCOME** Dogs welcome. Children over 14-years-old.

**ANY OTHER INFO** This pub is named after the founder of Winchester College, William of Wykeham. Rooms are stocked with Nelson memorabilia and old desks from Winchester College. Popular with locals. Sauna on site. Recommended by Egon Ronay, *The Good Hotel Guide*, *The Good Food Guide* and *The Good Pub Guide* Wine Pub of the Year 1998, *The Sunday Times* Golden Pillow award 1999.

**HOW TO GET THERE** The pub is by Kingsgate arch between the college and cathedral.

Kilverts Hotel, The Bullring, Hay-on-Wye, Herefordshire HR3 5AG
**Tel** 01497 821042 **Fax** 01497 821580 **website** www.hay-on-wye.co.uk/kilverts
**Star ratings** **AA/Welsh Tourist Board

**NO OF ROOMS** 11.

**COST** From £35 per night bed and breakfast for a single room. From £65 per night bed and breakfast for a double room.

**SPECIAL BREAKS/OFFERS** From £170 per person for two nights' dinner, bed and breakfast plus an extra night's stay charged at £80 per person.

**FOOD** Varied and extensive menu with emphasis on fresh local produce both in Colin Thomson's restaurant and the bar. Fresh fish a speciality. Extensive wine list. Selection real ales. Beer garden. Awarded an AA rosette.

**SPORT THAT CAN BE ARRANGED** Salmon and coarse fishing on the River Wye and Edw. Hunting with the Golden Valley, Brecon and Radnor and West Herefordshire Foxhounds. Also golf, pony trekking, cycling and canoeing.

**SEASONS/BEST TIMES FOR SPECIALIST SPORTS** Traditional seasons.

**DOGS/CHILDREN WELCOME** Dogs charged £5 per stay. Children over six who share their parents' room charged at £15 per night bed and breakfast.

**ANY OTHER INFO** Kilverts Hotel is owned and managed by Colin Thomson who is a shooting, hunting and racing enthusiast. Recommended by *The Good Pub Guide* 1999 and 2000. Popular with the locals. Drying room.

**HOW TO GET THERE** From London: M4 over Severn Bridge to junction 24. Take A449 then A40. Pass Crickhowell then take A479 to Talgarth. Turn on to A4079, then A438 and then B4350 to Hay-on-Wye. From Birmingham: M5 to junction 8. M50 to Ross-on-Wye. A49 to Hereford. After Harewood End turn left for Hay-on-Wye on B4348.

The Ancient Camp Inn, Ruckhall, Near Eaton Bishop, Herefordshire HR2 9QX
**Tel** 01981 250449 **Fax** 01981 251581
**Star ratings** **AA

**NO OF ROOMS** Five.

**COST** From £45 per night bed and breakfast for a single room. From £55.70 per night bed and breakfast for a double room.

**SPECIAL BREAKS/OFFERS** Winter: from £62 per night dinner, bed and breakfast for a single room. From £90 to £105 per night dinner, bed and breakfast for a double room.

**FOOD** Modern English cuisine using fresh local produce. Bar meals at lunch times. Nearly 60 bins on wine list. Real ale. Awarded two AA rosettes. Michelin Inn Restaurant of the Year 1998.

**SPORT ON OFFER/THAT CAN BE ARRANGED** Coarse fishing on the River Wye. Hunting with the South Herefordshire and Brecon Foxhounds. Golf locally.

**SEASONS/BEST TIMES FOR SPECIALIST SPORTS** Traditional seasons.

**DOGS/CHILDREN WELCOME** No.

**ANY OTHER INFO** Old country inn with open fires, flagstone floors, oak beams and views down across the valley to the River Wye. The pub's name is taken from the Iron Age hill fort which the Camp now covers. Originally the pub was a shop, then a forge and a cider house. It is now owned by Jason and Lisa Eland and Ewart and Pauline McKie. Very popular with locals – probably one of Herefordshire's best-kept eating secrets.

**LOCATION** Turn off main Hereford to Abergavenny road A465 to Ruckhall. Follow road for about 2½ miles to Ancient Camp.

The Red Lion Hotel, Bredwardine, Hereford, Herefordshire HR3 6BU
**Tel** 01981 500303 **Fax** 01981 500400 **website** www.hay-on-wye.co.uk/redlion

**NO OF ROOMS** 10.

**COST** From £29.50 per person per night bed and breakfast sharing a double/twin room.

**SPECIAL BREAKS/OFFERS** From £42 per person per night dinner, bed and breakfast sharing a double/twin room.

**FOOD** Restaurant and bar meals.

**SPORT ON OFFER/THAT CAN BE ARRANGED** Salmon, barbel and pike fishing on eight miles of the River Wye. Free salmon fishing between April and mid-June. Golf locally.

**SEASONS/BEST TIMES FOR SPECIALIST SPORTS** Salmon in the spring, barbel in the summer/autumn and pike in winter.

**DOGS/CHILDREN WELCOME** Yes.

**ANY OTHER INFO** Situated in the Wye Valley just seven miles from Hay-on-Wye, the famous second-hand book centre of the UK and host of *The Sunday Times* Hay Literary Festival.

**HOW TO GET THERE** Twelve miles from Hereford, just off A438, towards Hay-on-Wye and Brecon.

The Talbot, New Street, Ledbury, Herefordshire HR8 2DX
**Tel** 01531 632963 **Fax** 01531 633796
**e-mail** susan.talbot@dial.pipex.com **website** www.SmoothHound.co.uk/hotels/talbot.html
**Star ratings** **AA

**NO OF ROOMS** Seven.

**COST** From £44.50 per night for a double room (room only). Single occupancy from £34.50 Monday to Thursday.

**SPECIAL BREAKS/OFFERS** Four nights for the price of three.

**FOOD** Fresh local produce used where possible, especially Herefordshire beef and vegetables. Varied menu. Very select wine list. Local guest beers. Popular with shooting parties.

**SPORT ON OFFER/THAT CAN BE ARRANGED** Hunting with the Ledbury Foxhounds who have their Boxing Day meet in the town centre. Also golf and racing.

**SEASONS/BEST TIMES FOR SPECIALIST SPORTS** Traditional seasons.

**DOGS/CHILDREN WELCOME** Yes.

**ANY OTHER INFO** The Talbot is a 16th-century coaching inn. The oak-panelled dining-room was once the scene of fighting between the Cavaliers and Roundheads.

**HOW TO GET THERE** Centre of Ledbury.

Ashford Castle, Cong, Co Mayo, Ireland
**Tel** 00 353 9246003 **Fax** 00 353 9246260
**e-mail** ashford@ashford.ie **website** www.ashford.ie
**Star ratings** *****AA

**NO OF ROOMS** 83.

**COST** From IR£284 per night bed and breakfast for a double/twin room. Golf and health centre complementary to hotel residents.

**SPECIAL BREAKS/OFFERS** From IR£250 per person sharing a double room including two nights' bed and breakfast and one evening dinner. Available from 1 November to 22 December and 2 January to 31 March. Mark Phillips riding course (November) from IR£2,750 per person to include black tie dinner, accommodation, meals, clinic, hunting caps and hirelings.

**FOOD** Two dining-rooms: George V dining-room with traditional cuisine; and the Connaught Room gourmet restaurant. Both menus rely on fresh local produce such as oysters, fish, lamb, foie gras, beef and locally grown herbs. Extensive wine list caters for all markets.

**SPORT ON OFFER/THAT CAN BE ARRANGED** Salmon, brown trout, pike and perch fishing in Lough Corrib. Salmon, brown trout and sea-trout fishing on the River Cong. Gillies, boats and tuition available. Sea-trout and salmon fishing can also be arranged in Connemara. Archery and clay pigeon shooting. Hunting with Galway Blazers. Falconry, lake cruises, pony and trap rides, cycling, golf and tennis. Leisure centre. Equestrian centre with a week-long course run by Capt Mark Phillips.

**SEASONS/BEST TIMES FOR SPECIALIST SPORTS** Fishing: March to September.

**DOGS/CHILDREN WELCOME** No dogs in the hotel. Children welcome.

**ANY OTHER INFO** Ashford Castle is set within 350 acres of woodland and formal gardens on the edge of Ireland's second largest lake, Lough Corrib. It was once Lord Ardilaun and the Guinness family's country estate. Richly decorated with objets d'art. The Connaught Room features a unique and priceless hand-crafted inglenook reaching 20ft to the oak ceiling. Before and after dinner guests are entertained by a harpist or pianist in the Dungeon Bar. Billiards room, gym, whirlpool, steam room, sauna, tennis courts, indoor riding arena and a cross-country course. Boutique.

**HOW TO GET THERE** Fly direct to Shannon or Knock.

Ballynahinch Castle Hotel, Recess, Co Galway, Ireland
**Tel** 00 353 9531006 **Fax** 00 353 9531085 **e-mail** bhinch@iol.ie
**Star ratings** ****AA

**NO OF ROOMS** 40.

**COST** From IR£130 to IR£250 per night bed and breakfast in a double room.

**FOOD** Classic dishes in the style of Irish country house and French cuisine. Fresh fish and game specialities. Extensive and varied wine list. Good selection of both Irish and Scottish malt whiskies. Awarded two AA rosettes.

**SPORT ON OFFER/THAT CAN BE ARRANGED** Salmon and sea-trout fishing on private beats, and lake within the Ballynahinch Fishery. Sea fishing from Clifden. Also sailing and riding. Woodcock-shooting over 13,000 acres. Clay pigeon shooting. Own tennis court.

**SEASONS/BEST TIMES FOR SPECIALIST SPORTS** Fishing: 1 February to 30 September, best June to September. Shooting: November, December and January.

**DOGS/CHILDREN WELCOME** No dogs. Children are welcome but the hotel is not geared for them.

**ANY OTHER INFO** Ballynahinch is set within a 350-acre private estate. Pirate queen married Donal O'Flaherty in 1529 and came to live at the castle. It was then rebuilt in the 18th century and owned by, among many, the Indian cricketer Maharajah Ranjitsinhji.

**HOW TO GET THERE** N59 west from Galway. After Recess village turn left to Ballynahinch and Roundstone.

Ballyvolane House, Castlelyons, Co Cork, Ireland
**Tel** 00 353 2536349 **Fax** 00 353 2536781
**e-mail** ballyvol@iol.ie **website** www.ballyvolanehouse.ie
**Star ratings** AA Five Diamonds

**NO OF ROOMS** Six.

**COST** From IR£38 to IR£50.00 per person per night bed and breakfast for a double/twin room based on two people sharing. Single supplement IR£12.

**FOOD** Country-house cooking. Communal dining table although there are two smaller tables for those who would rather dine alone.

**SPORT ON OFFER/THAT CAN BE ARRANGED** Salmon fishing on the hotel's own eight miles of the River Blackwater. Gillies and tuition available. Rainbow trout in stocked lakes. Also sea fishing, riding, tennis and golf.

**SEASONS/BEST TIMES FOR SPECIALIST SPORTS** 1 February to 30 September.

**DOGS/CHILDREN WELCOME** Children welcome. Dogs in cars only.

**ANY OTHER INFO** Ballyvolane House was built in 1728 and renovated 120 years later in Italianate style. Extensive gardens including formal terraces and bluebell woodland walks where there is an on-going tree planting programme. Recommended by *The Good Hotel Guide.*

**HOW TO GET THERE** From Cork, turn right off N8 on to R628 at the River Bride just before Rathcormac. Follow signs to the house.

Blackwater Lodge, Upper Ballyduff, Co Waterford, Ireland
**Tel** 00 353 5860235 **Fax** 00 353 5860162
**e-mail** bwlodge@indigo.ie **website** www.blackwaterlodge.net
**Star ratings** *Irish Tourist Board

**NO OF ROOMS** 23.

**COST** From IR£21 to IR£50 per person per night bed and breakfast based on two people sharing a double room.

**FOOD** Both à la carte and table d'hôte menus available in the restaurant. Own-smoked salmon and chicken a speciality. About 40 bins offered on the wine list.

**SPORT ON OFFER/THAT CAN BE ARRANGED** Salmon fishing on the Lodge's private and exclusive 15 miles of the River Blackwater. Fishing charged from IR£35 to IR£60 per rod per day. Gillies available.

**SEASONS/BEST TIMES FOR SPECIALIST SPORTS** Salmon: 1 February to 30 September. Best times from June onwards.

**DOGS/CHILDREN WELCOME** Yes.

**ANY OTHER INFO** Blackwater Lodge controls 16 beats (about 15 miles of fishing) on the reaches of the river between Lismore and Mallow. This covers some 40 river miles, starting only three miles above the tidal limit. The Lodge overlooks the river and the bar has views over the Blackwater. Tackle shop and smokery. The Lodge's website updates the river report daily.

**HOW TO GET THERE** The Lodge is situated between Fermoy and Lismore on the border between counties Cork and Waterford. It is only one hour from Cork, two hours from Shannon and Rosslare and four hours from Dublin. The Lodge can arrange car ferry tickets from the UK at excellent rates or hire cars from airports.

Camillaun/Corrib County Angling Centre, Eighterard, Oughterard, Co Galway, Ireland
**Tel** 00 353 91552678 **Fax** 00 353 91552439
**e-mail** camillaun@eircom.net **website** http://homepage.eircom.net/~camillaunfishing

**NO OF ROOMS** Five.

**COST** From IR£20 per person per night bed and breakfast based on two people sharing a double room.

**FOOD** Dinner taken in a single sitting round a table. Fresh local produce used in season. Fish a speciality. Manager Deirdre Forde used to run her own restaurant in town.

**SPORT ON OFFER/THAT CAN BE ARRANGED** Salmon and wild brown trout fishing on Lough Corrib. Salmon fishing at Connemara fisheries. Golf locally.

**SEASONS/BEST TIMES FOR SPECIALIST SPORTS** March to June and September.

**DOGS/CHILDREN WELCOME** Yes.

**ANY OTHER INFO** Greg and Deirdre Forde manage this small friendly bed and breakfast which has magnificent views across the River Owenriff. Oughterard is the angling capital of Lough Corrib. Large boat house with rod racks and drying facilities.

**HOW TO GET THERE** Take N59 out of Galway. Oughterard is the second village. Turn right at the Lake Hotel over the bridge and take the next right.

Careysville, Fermoy, Co Cork, Ireland
**Tel** 00 353 2531712 **Fax** 00 353 5854896 **e-mail** lismoreestates@tinet.ie

**NO OF ROOMS** Six.

**COST** From IR£800 per person per week for accommodation. Fishing is extra and costs between IR£550 and IR£1,500 per rod per week according to the season.

**SPECIAL BREAKS/OFFERS** During August.

**FOOD** Traditional Irish prepared using fresh local produce. Meals included in price. Lunch served by the river in the fishing hut (once a cricket pavilion).

**SPORT ON OFFER/THAT CAN BE ARRANGED** Salmon fishing on the Careysville beat of the Munster Blackwater. Almost two miles of double-bank fishing producing an average 606 salmon per season. Racing at Mallow, Thurles, Clonmel and Tipperary. Golf.

**SEASONS/BEST TIMES FOR SPECIALIST SPORTS** 1 February to 30 September; February and March best for spring salmon, June to mid July for grilse.

**DOGS/CHILDREN WELCOME** Yes.

**ANY OTHER INFO** Careysville is late Georgian and built on a high escarpment on the site of Ballymacpatrick Castle overlooking the Munster Blackwater. Large drying room and freezer for guests to store their salmon. Also a salmon smoking service.

**HOW TO GET THERE** From the main square in Fermoy take N72 east to Tallow. After nearly two miles turn left for just over a mile through Clondulane. Gateway to Careysville is on the left. Reservations can also be made by calling Michael Penruddock at Lismore Castle on 00 353 5854424.

Castle Oaks House Hotel, Castleconnell, Co Limerick, Ireland
**Tel** 00 353 61377666 **Fax** 00 353 61377717
**e-mail** info@castle-oaks.com **website** www.castle-oaks.com
**Star ratings** ***Irish Tourist Board Grade A

**NO OF ROOMS** 20.

**COST** From IR£44 per person per night bed and breakfast based on two people sharing.

**SPECIAL BREAKS/OFFERS** From IR£105 per person sharing a double room for two nights' bed and breakfast and one evening meal.

**FOOD** Bar and restaurant menus. Emphasis on Irish country house cooking. Extensive wine list. Selection Irish malt whiskies. Awarded two AA rosettes. Egon Ronay recommended.

**SPORT ON OFFER/THAT CAN BE ARRANGED** Trout and salmon fishing on the Rivers Shannon, Mulcair, Newport and Fergus. Tuition available. Also swimming, tennis and basketball.

**SEASONS/BEST TIMES FOR SPECIALIST SPORTS** April to September.

**DOGS/CHILDREN WELCOME** No dogs. Children welcome.

**ANY OTHER INFO** The Castle Oaks House, owned by Michael Fagan, is an 18th-Georgian country house on a 26-acre estate fronting the banks of the River Shannon. Tackle hire and repair service. Indoor heated swimming pool. Also sauna, jacuzzi, steam room, gym and tennis court.

**HOW TO GET THERE** Seven miles outside Limerick city off N7 (Dublin road).

Clonanav Fly Fishing Centre and School, Nire Valley, Ballymacarby, Clonmel, Co Waterford, Ireland
**Tel** 00 353 52 36141 **Fax** 00 353 52 36294
**e-mail** andrew@flyfishingireland.com **website** www.flyfishingireland.com
**Star ratings** ***Irish Tourist Board

**NO OF ROOMS** 14.

**COST** From IR£30 to IR£35 per night bed and breakfast for a double room.

**FOOD** Evening meals, which are wholesome and homemade, are served on request. Selection of fine wines. Good food available in local pubs and restaurants.

**SPORT ON OFFER/THAT CAN BE ARRANGED** Brown trout on the Rivers Suir, Nire and Tar. Approved fly-fishing school with instructor Andrew Ryan. Catch-and-release policy. Salmon fishing in the Munster Blackwater. Wild brown trout fishing in Nire Lakes, Rivers Anner and Duag. Tench and rudd fishing on Lake Dromana. Pike fishing on Lake Belle. Roach and dace at Cappoquin. Sea fishing from Dungarvan and Helvick. Also riding, golf and tennis locally.

**SEASONS/BEST TIMES FOR SPECIALIST SPORTS** Trout: May to September. Salmon: August and September.

**DOGS/CHILDREN WELCOME** No dogs. Children welcome.

**ANY OTHER INFO** Clonanav (meaning Ox meadow in Gaelic) is situated in the scenic Nire Valley in between the Comeragh and Knockmealdown mountains. Private fisheries and hotel run by Larry and Eileen Ryan and their family. Fishing tackle shop. Tackle hire. Casting green and beginners' lake. Own tennis court. Cottage to let.

**HOW TO GET THERE** Fly either to Cork or Dublin. By car Clonanav is 1½ hours from Cork, three hours from Dublin and two hours from Shannon. Ballymacarby is situated between Dungarvan and Clonmel.

Delphi Lodge, Leenane, Co Galway, Ireland
**Tel** 00 353 9542222 **Fax** 00 353 9542296 **e-mail** delfish@iol.ie

**NO OF ROOMS** 12.

**COST** From IR£40 to IR£80 per person per night bed and breakfast based on two people sharing a double room. The more expensive rooms are large and overlook the lake.

**SPECIAL BREAKS/OFFERS** Three-day full board package from IR£195 to IR£295 per person.

**FOOD** Eclectic country-house style. Extensive wine list. Set meals around a large oak dining-room table.

**SPORT ON OFFER/THAT CAN BE ARRANGED** Salmon and sea-trout fishing on the Delphi fishery. Limited to 12 rods either bank fishing on the River Bundorragha or boat fishing on two lakes. Gillies available. Fly-fishing tuition weekends held five times a year.

**SEASONS/BEST TIMES FOR SPECIALIST SPORTS** Spring salmon: February to May; sea-trout: July to September; grilse: June and July.

**DOGS/CHILDREN WELCOME** No.

**ANY OTHER INFO** Delphi Lodge is an 1830s country house owned by Peter Mantle, himself an enthusiastic fly-fisher. The house was formerly the sporting base for the Marquis of Sligo. It stands at the base of Connemara's tallest mountains in a remote and unspoilt valley overlooking a lake. Well-stocked library. Billiards room.

**HOW TO GET THERE** Delphi Lodge is eight miles north of Leenane, 50 miles north west of Galway, and 20 miles south west of Westport. It is marked on most maps.

Dromoland Castle, Newmarket-on-Fergus, Co Clare, Ireland
**Tel** 00 353 61368144 **Fax** 00 353 61363355 **e-mail** res@dromoland.ie
**Star ratings** *****AA

**NO OF ROOMS** 100.

**COST** From IR£140 to IR£368 per room per night bed and breakfast.

**SPECIAL BREAKS/OFFERS** From £250 per person including two nights' bed and breakfast and one dinner (from November to March).

**FOOD** European-style cuisine in Earl of Thomond dining-room. Brasserie dining in the club house's Fig Tree restaurant. Emphasis on fresh local produce especially fish, lamb and beef. Extensive and varied wine list. Mrs White's traditional afternoon tea is a speciality.

**SPORT ON OFFER/THAT CAN BE ARRANGED** Game-shooting on the estate. Trout fishing on Lake Dromoland. Clay pigeon shooting. Also riding, golf, archery, swimming, cycling and off-road driving. Leisure centre.

**SEASONS/BEST TIMES FOR SPECIALIST SPORTS** Traditional seasons.

**DOGS/CHILDREN WELCOME** No dogs. Children welcome.

**ANY OTHER INFO** Dromoland is the ancestral home of the O'Briens, barons of Inchiquin and direct descendants of Brian Boru – High King of Ireland. It is surrounded by over 360 acres of wooded parkland. Family portraits line the oak-panelled hall and stairways; sporting trophies the gallery. A 300-year-old stone gateway leads to a 17th-century walled garden. Also sauna, steam bath, gym and indoor swimming pool.

**HOW TO GET THERE** Eight miles from Shannon.

Fermoyle Lodge, Costello, Co Galway, Ireland
**Tel** 00 353 91786111 **Fax** 00 353 91786154
**e-mail** fermoylelodge@eircom.net **website** www.fermoylelodge.com

**NO OF ROOMS** Six.

**COST** From IR£45 per person per night bed and breakfast in a double room based on two people sharing.

**FOOD** Three-course dinner using home-grown or local produce wherever possible. Seafood a speciality.

**SPORT ON OFFER/THAT CAN BE ARRANGED** Salmon and sea- and brown trout fishing on the Costello and Fermoyle Fisheries. Choice of river or lake fishing for salmon and sea-trout. Lake fishing for sea-reared rainbow trout. Brown trout fishing on Lough Corrib. Gillies and tuition available. Sea fishing from Clifden and Rossaveal harbours. Also golf and riding.

**SEASONS/BEST TIMES FOR SPECIALIST SPORTS** Brown trout: April and May; salmon: June and September; and sea-trout: July, August and September.

**DOGS/CHILDREN WELCOME** Not suitable.

**ANY OTHER INFO** Fermoyle Lodge was originally built as a sporting lodge by the Berridge family in 1875. It is situated in one of Connemara's most wild and remote parts. The lodge is surrounded by rhododendrons and woodland and commands views over Fermoyle Lake to the distant Twelve Pins.

**HOW TO GET THERE** From Galway take N59 towards Clifden. In Oughterard turn left just before bridge and follow signs for Costello. Fermoyle Lodge is 11 miles from Oughterard on right.

Humewood Castle, Humewood, Kiltegan, Co Wicklow, Ireland
**Tel** 00 353 50873215 **Fax** 00 353 50873382 **e-mail** humewood@iol.ie
**Star ratings** *****AA

**NO OF ROOMS** 13.

**COST** From IR£360 (low season) to IR£420 (high season) per night bed and breakfast per suite. Also two-bedroomed lodge to let.

**FOOD** Fine dining. Meals are prepared using fresh local produce with vegetables supplied from a local organic garden. Extensive wine list and large selection of Irish and Scottish malt whiskies.

**SPORT ON OFFER/THAT CAN BE ARRANGED** Clay pigeon shooting. Salmon and trout fishing on the River Slaney and local lakes. Gillies available. Stalking on the estate. Pheasant- and duck-shooting on the estate. Hunting with the Kildare, Kilkenny, The Island, Shillelagh and Ward Union Foxhounds. Riding lessons with Nini Odenrick, chef d'équipe of the Irish Dressage team. Also polo, golf, cycling and falconry.

**SEASONS/BEST TIMES FOR SPECIALIST SPORTS** Traditional seasons.

**DOGS/CHILDREN WELCOME** No dogs. Children welcome.

**ANY OTHER INFO** Humewood was commissioned by William White in the 1860s and was a hunting lodge for the Hume family. It is set within 440 acres and lends itself to the style of the country house hotel. Each bedroom is individually designed and the house is furnished with antiques and works of art. Also billiards room and tennis court.

**HOW TO GET THERE** From Dublin airport take M1 to Dublin. Turn right on to M50 and then N81 to Baltinglass. Take R747 to Hacketstown. Turn left into Kiltegan and follow the road to the castle.

Lough Inagh Lodge Hotel, Recess, Connemara, Co Galway, Ireland
**Tel** 00 353 9534706 **Fax** 00 353 9534708
**e-mail** inagh@iol.ie **website** www.commerce.ie/inagh
**Star ratings** ***AA

**NO OF ROOMS** 12.

**COST** From IR£55 (low season) to IR£68.20 (high season) per person per night bed and breakfast in a double room based on two people sharing.

**SPECIAL BREAKS/OFFERS** From IR£119.90 (low season) to IR£170.50 (high season) per person for two nights' bed and breakfast and one dinner, based on two people sharing a double room.

**FOOD** Irish cuisine with French flair. Seafood a speciality. Extensive wine list with leanings toward the New World and traditional French. Good selection Irish and Scottish malt whiskies.

**SPORT ON OFFER/THAT CAN BE ARRANGED** Salmon, sea- and brown trout fishing on the Lough Inagh system and River Derryclare. Also Sea fishing and hill walking.

**SEASONS/BEST TIMES FOR SPECIALIST SPORTS** Salmon: June to September.

**DOGS/CHILDREN WELCOME** Yes.

**ANY OTHER INFO** Lough Inagh Lodge was originally the fishing and shooting lodge of the Martins family who sold it to the Berridges, an English brewing family. Eleven years ago it became a hotel. It borders Connemara National Park.

**HOW TO GET THERE** Fly to Shannon. Lough Inagh is 2½ hours from there.

Mount Juliet, Thomastown, Co Kilkenny, Ireland
**Tel** 00 353 5673000 **Fax** 00 353 5673019
**e-mail** info@mountjuliet.ie **website** www.mountjuliet.ie
**Star ratings** ****AA

**NO OF ROOMS** 59.

**COST** From IR£115 per person per night for a double room. Breakfast IR£12.50 per person.

**SPECIAL BREAKS/OFFERS** Midweek break: from IR£165 per person based on two people sharing a double room including two nights' accommodation, two full Irish breakfasts and one dinner. Midweek spa break: from IR£225 per person based on two people sharing a double room including two night's midweek accommodation, two full Irish breakfasts, one dinner and a choice of a back massage or reflexology on both days.

**FOOD** Fine dining in the restaurant in Mount Juliet House. Bar and restaurant menus in the President's bar in the Hunters Yard. A la carte menu in Kendals Restaurant in the Hunters Yard. Extensive wine list. Selection Irish and Scottish malt whiskies. Awarded RAC Gold Ribbon for excellence.

**SPORT ON OFFER/THAT CAN BE ARRANGED** Salmon and brown trout fishing on the estate's own beat of King's River which is a tributary of the River Nore. Tuition and gillies available. Hunting available seven days a weeks. Also riding, archery, clay pigeon shooting, golf, tennis and swimming.

**SEASONS/BEST TIMES FOR SPECIALIST SPORTS** Fishing: March to September.

**DOGS/CHILDREN WELCOME** No dogs. Children welcome.

**ANY OTHER INFO** The Mount Juliet estate was originally two separate estates, Walton's Grove and Ballylinch. The Waltons owned Walton's Grove until William Walton was dispossessed by Cromwell. Later it became James II's and then Mr Kendall's. He was robbed by highwaymen who take off him an important portfolio. He begged Revd Thomas Bushe to retrieve it, which he did. Kendall was so grateful he left all his property to the Revd who duly squandered it all. He sold Kendall's Grove to the Earl of Carrick who owned neighbouring Ballylinch. The estate was then named after his wife, Lady Juliana, always known as Juliet. There's a tennis court, indoor swimming pool, gym, steam room, sauna and beauty salon. AA Hotel of the Year 1999.

**HOW TO GET THERE** M7 from Dublin. M9 towards Waterford. N9 toward Carlow and Gowran to Thomastown.

Newport House, Newport, Co Mayo, Ireland
**Tel** 00 353 9841222 **Fax** 00 353 9841613
**e-mail** kjt1@anu.ie

**NO OF ROOMS** 18.

**COST** From IR£63 per person per night bed and breakfast (low season). From IR£66 to IR£82 per person per night bed and breakfast (high season). Rates are based on two people sharing a double room.

**FOOD** French and country-house style cuisine using fresh produce from the hotel's own fishery, garden and farm. Home-smoked salmon and fresh seafood a speciality. Extensive cellar including many classic vintages.

**SPORT ON OFFER/THAT CAN BE ARRANGED** Salmon and sea-trout fishing on eight miles of the River Newport and Lough Beltra. Salmon fishing on Lochs Feeagh, Furnace, Conn and Mask. Lochs Feeagh and Furnace are the site of the Salmon Research Trust of Ireland installations and laboratories. Sea angling. Game-shooting over 2,000 acres. Also swimming, diving, golf, pony trekking and hang gliding.

**SEASONS/BEST TIMES FOR SPECIALIST SPORTS** Fishing: 20 March to end September.

**DOGS/CHILDREN WELCOME** Children welcome. Dogs only in the annexe.

**ANY OTHER INFO** This historic Georgian house set within its own gardens and parkland overlooking the River Newport and quay was, for 200 years, the home of the O'Donnells, once the Earls of Tir Connell. The house is furnished with antiques and fine art. Billiards room.

**HOW TO GET THERE** Fly from Stansted to Knock. Newport is an hour from Knock. Dublin to Newport four hours' drive.

Pontoon Bridge Hotel, Pontoon, Foxford, Co Mayo, Ireland
**Tel** 00 353 9456120 **Fax** 00 353 9456688
**e-mail** fishing@pontoonbridge.com **website** www.pontoonbridge.com
**Star ratings** ***AA

**NO OF ROOMS** 40.

**COST** From IR£65 per person per night bed and breakfast based on two people sharing a double room.

**SPECIAL BREAKS/OFFERS** Kingdom of Conn Special: from IR£249 per person Sunday to Thursday, five nights' bed and breakfast and four gourmet dinners. Fly-fishing, painting and cookery courses.

**FOOD** Fine dining in the Twin Lakes restaurant. Bar bistro. Both menus large and varied using fresh local produce where possible. Wine list offers 65 bins.

**SPORT ON OFFER/THAT CAN BE ARRANGED** Salmon fishing on River Moy. Wild brown trout, salmon and perch in Loughs Conn and Cullin. Sea fishing at Clew Bay and Killala. New leisure centre opening late 2000.

**SEASONS/BEST TIMES FOR SPECIALIST SPORTS** Trout: May, June and September. Salmon: April, July to September.

**DOGS/CHILDREN WELCOME** Yes.

**ANY OTHER INFO** Pontoon Bridge, situated on the narrow peninsula between Loughs Conn and Cullin, has been a hotel for over 100 years. It has belonged to the Geary family since 1964 and is currently under the charge of Brendan and Ann Geary. Son John Geary edits the hotel's in-house fishing magazine, *The Kingdom Of Conn*. Alan Pearson runs one-, two- and four-day fly-fishing courses from the hotel. There are also landscape painting courses taken by Pat Goff and cookery courses which run during specific weeks . These are taken by Mary Geary, the hotel's chef when she isn't captaining the Irish ladies fly-fishing team as she has for four years. The hotel has featured on BBC's *Holiday* programme and ITV's *Wish You Were Here.*

**HOW TO GET THERE** Direct flights from Stansted and Manchester to Knock which is only 20 minutes from the hotel.

The Glencar House Hotel, Glencar, Co Kerry, Ireland
**Tel** 00 353 669760102 **Fax** 00 353 669760167
**e-mail** glencarh@iol.ie **website** www.glencarhouse.com
**Star ratings** **AA

**NO OF ROOMS** 18.

**COST** From IR£42 to IR£55 per person per night bed and breakfast based on two people sharing a double room.

**SPECIAL BREAKS/OFFERS** From IR£581 per person for one week's fishing, dinner, bed and breakfast.

**FOOD** Traditional Irish using fresh local produce specialising in roasts, steaks and fish. Extensive wine list.

**SPORT ON OFFER/THAT CAN BE ARRANGED** Salmon fishing on the hotel's own 10 miles of the Upper Caragh. Two private and one public lake.

**SEASONS/BEST TIMES FOR SPECIALIST SPORTS** Spring Salmon: 1 February to 15 May. Grilse: 15 May to 30 September.

**DOGS/CHILDREN WELCOME** Yes.

**ANY OTHER INFO** Glencar House Hotel, owned by Kevin Factor, was built as a hunting lodge in the late 1670s by the Earl of Landsdowne, William Petty. It is set in the highlands of Kerry and surrounded by ancient woodland. The MacGillycuddy's Reeks and Glencar are now classified as a Special Area of Conservation.

**HOW TO GET THERE** From Killarney follow signs in Killorglin. Turn left after the bridge in town and follow signs to the hotel.

The Kildare Hotel And Country Club, Straffan, Co Kildare, Ireland
**Tel** 00 353 16017200 **Fax** 00 353 16017299
**e-mail** sales@kclub.ie **website** www.kclub.ie
**Star ratings** *****AA Red/RAC Gold Ribbon

**NO OF ROOMS** 62.

**COST** From IR£310 to IR£1,000 per room per night (room only).

**SPECIAL BREAKS/OFFERS** From IR£350 per person sharing a double room, including two nights' accommodation, two full Irish breakfasts, two rounds of golf or a leisure activity such as fishing. Break to be taken from November to March.

**FOOD** Two restaurants. French cuisine with an Irish interpretation. Vegetables, herbs and fruit grown in the hotel's own Victorian walled garden. Extensive fine wine list. Large selection Irish and Scottish malt whiskies. Awarded four AA rosettes.

**SPORT ON OFFER/THAT CAN BE ARRANGED** Salmon and trout fishing on a mile stretch of the River Liffey. Gillies and tuition available. Stocked brown trout, carp, bream, tench and rudd in five lakes. All equipment provided. Clay pigeon shooting. Driven pheasant- shooting in the Naire Valley. Hunting with the Kildare and Mead Foxhounds. Riding. The Curragh, Punchestown, Leopardstown and Naas racecourses are just 30 minutes' drive away. Health and leisure centre. Also squash, swimming, tennis, cycling and boating.

**SEASONS/BEST TIMES FOR SPECIALIST SPORTS** River fishing: January to September. Driven-shooting: November to February.

**DOGS/CHILDREN WELCOME** Yes.

**ANY OTHER INFO** The Kildare is a restored Georgian estate set within 300 acres. The hotel houses over 600 tapestries, as well as antiques and paintings by the likes of Orpen and Lavery. One room is dedicated to Jack B Yeats' paintings. Gardens run along the River Liffey, on to Inismor Island and through a walled garden. Two indoor and outdoor courts. Also squash court, gym, jacuzzi, sauna and massage. Home of the Smurfit European Open and the 2005 Ryder Cup matches. Egon Ronay Irish Hotel of the Year 1997.

**HOW TO GET THERE** The hotel is 30 minutes south west of Dublin airport, 45 minutes from the city centre off N7.

The George Hotel, Quay Street, Yarmouth, Isle of Wight PO41 0PE
**Tel** 01983 760331 **Fax** 01983 760425
**e-mail** res@thegeorge.co.uk **website** www.thegeorge.co.uk
**Star ratings** ***AA Red

**NO OF ROOMS** 17.

**COST** From £85 per night bed and breakfast for a single room. From £145 to £192 per night bed and breakfast for a double/twin room.

**SPECIAL BREAKS/OFFERS** From £185 to £232 per night for two people for two days' dinner, bed and breakfast. Shooting parties: from £97.50 dinner, bed and breakfast for a single room. From £160 dinner, bed and breakfast for a double room. Rates apply Sunday to Thursday.

**FOOD** Brasserie serves Modern European Food. Fine dining in the restaurant which has a Michelin star. Over 300 bins available on the wine list which has a large selection of old clarets.

**SPORT ON OFFER/THAT CAN BE ARRANGED** Pheasant-shooting on the island. Also sea fishing and sailing.

**SEASONS/BEST TIMES FOR SPECIALIST SPORTS** Traditional seasons.

**DOGS/CHILDREN WELCOME** Yes, by prior arrangement.

**ANY OTHER INFO** The George is a 17th-century town house a few paces from the harbour. It was formerly the island's Governor's residence. Gun cabinets in most bedrooms. Private beach. Motor yacht for hire.

**HOW TO GET THERE** The Lymington to Yarmouth ferry takes about 30 minutes.

The Inn At Whitewell, Forest of Bowland, near Clitheroe, Lancashire BB7 3AT
**Tel** 01200 448222 **Fax** 01200 448298
**Star ratings** ****AA

**NO OF ROOMS** 17.

**COST** From £57 per night bed and breakfast for a single room. From £80 per night bed and breakfast for a double room.

**FOOD** Good fresh English/Classical style. Fresh fish and game on both restaurant and bar menus. A wine merchant shares the premises so the wine list is unusually extensive.

**SPORT ON OFFER/THAT CAN BE ARRANGED** Salmon, brown and sea-trout and grayling fishing on the hotel's own five miles, both banks, of the River Hodder. Fishing from £17 to £37 per rod per day. Grayling £10 per rod per day. Pheasant-shooting can be arranged for teams of guns on local shoots. Grouse-shooting on Abbeystead, Keasden, Lancashire and Brennand moors. Also golf.

**SEASONS/BEST TIMES FOR SPECIALIST SPORTS** Salmon, brown and rainbow trout: 15 March to 31 October. Grayling: 1 November to 14 March.

**DOGS/CHILDREN WELCOME** Dogs welcome anywhere except the restaurant. Cats welcome but in the interests of soft furnishings the hotel would be happier if male cats are no longer active lovers. Children who are not bawling welcome anywhere.

**ANY OTHER INFO** The inn sits in the Forest of Bowland on the banks of the River Hodder. The earliest parts of the building date back to the 1300s and the keeper of the forest used to live here in what would have then been the manor house. Peat fires in some bedrooms. Antiques and prints found throughout the inn. Art gallery on premises.

**HOW TO GET THERE** From the south: leave M6 at junction 31A. Head for Longridge and then follow signs to Whitewell. From the north: leave M6 at Forton services and follow signs through the Trough of Bowland. From the east: leave A59 at Clitheroe, head for Edisford Bridge then follow signs to Whitewell. From the west: leave A59 for Whalley and follow signs to Mitton and Whitewell.

Stapleford Park, Near Melton Mowbray, Leicestershire LE14 2EF
**Tel** 01572 787522 **Fax** 01572 787651
**e-mail** reservations@stapleford.co.uk **website** www.stapleford.co.uk
**Star ratings** ****AA Red

**NO OF ROOMS** 51.

**COST** From £165 to £495 per night bed and breakfast for a double room. Prices exclude VAT.

**SPECIAL BREAKS/OFFERS** Please enquire.

**FOOD** Fresh local produce used where possible. Rutland sausages and mash, Melton Mowbray pork pies and Stilton dips are Stapleford specialities. Extensive wine list. Selection of fine malts and brandies. Awarded two AA rosettes.

**SPORT ON OFFER/THAT CAN BE ARRANGED** Hunting with the Quorn, Cottesmore, Belvoir and Fernie. Livery by arrangement. Pheasant-shooting on local estates such as the Belvoir. Trout fishing on the park's own lake. Clay pigeon shooting. Also tennis, riding, swimming, gym, falconry, off-road driving and golf.

**SEASONS/BEST TIMES FOR SPECIALIST SPORTS** Traditional seasons.

**DOGS/CHILDREN WELCOME** Dogs charged £5 per night. Children sharing their parents' room charged £30 per night.

**ANY OTHER INFO** Stapleford Park was bought in 1996 by Peter de Savary. It is set within 500 acres of wood and parkland designed by Capability Brown. Originally it was bought by Lord Gretton, a successful brewer, to entertain his friends. It was then bought by the American businessman Bob Payton who refurbished the house as a country house hotel. Bedrooms have been decorated by designers such as Tricia Guild, David Hicks and Nina Campbell. Other rooms adorned with antiques, works of art, sporting trophies and grand design features. Stapleford is an outpost for the Carnegie Club. Clarins Spa and Beauty treatments. Treatment rooms display trompe l'oeil paintings by local muralist Jenny Bell. Indoor swimming pool, jacuzzi, tennis court and billiards room. Victorian stable block.

**HOW TO GET THERE** A1 to Colsterworth roundabout. Turn left on to B676 through Saxby then turn left for the hotel. M1 to junction 21a (if travelling north) junction 22 (if travelling south) then B676 and the hotel is six miles east of Melton Mowbray.

The Old White Hart Inn, 51 Main Street, Lyddington, Rutland, Leicestershire LE15 9LR
**Tel** 01572 821703 **Fax** 01572 821965

**NO OF ROOMS** Five.

**COST** From £45 per night bed and breakfast for a single room. From £65 per night bed and breakfast for a double room.

**FOOD** Extensive and varied menu and specials board. Emphasis on fresh local produce using fruit, vegetables and herbs from the pub's own gardens. All food homemade. Seafood a speciality. Comprehensive wine list. *The Good Pub Guide*'s Dining Pub of the Year 2000.

**SPORT ON OFFER/THAT CAN BE ARRANGED** Hunting with the Cottesmore, Quorn and Fernie Foxhounds. Pheasant- and partridge-shooting locally. Petanque. Coarse fishing on Eyebrook Reservoir and Rutland Water. Motor racing at Corby Speedway. Well situated for East of England Coursing Club and Burghley three-day event.

**SEASONS/BEST TIMES FOR SPECIALIST SPORTS** Traditional seasons.

**DOGS/CHILDREN WELCOME** Dogs outside only. Children welcome.

**ANY OTHER INFO** This is one of the few remaining traditional country pubs within the area. It is a 17th-century coaching inn which has retained its wooden beams and open fires. Stuart and Holly East bought it in 1997 when they left the Stone Trough in Kirkham Abbey. Popular with the locals.

**HOW TO GET THERE** Turn right on to B670 off A47 east of Uppingham towards Peterborough. Turn right for Lyddington.

Lady Anne's Hotel, St Martin's, Stamford, Lincolnshire PE9 2LJ
**Tel** 01780 481184 **Fax** 01780 765422
**Star ratings** ***AA

**NO OF ROOMS** 29.

**COST** From £52 per night bed and breakfast for a single room. From £68 to £90 per night bed and breakfast for a double room.

**FOOD** A la carte and table d'hôte menus in restaurant. Bar snacks available in the sitting-room, bar, garden room and garden. Roasts and Sunday lunch are specialities. Extensive wine list.

**SPORT ON OFFER/THAT CAN BE ARRANGED** Hunting with the Fernie, Quorn, Belvoir and Cottesmore Foxhounds. Fishing on the Rivers Nene and Wealand. Game-shooting on local estates. Also tennis, swimming, clay pigeon shooting, golf, laser shooting and off-road driving.

**SEASONS/BEST TIMES FOR SPECIALIST SPORTS** Traditional seasons.

**DOGS/CHILDREN WELCOME** Dogs by prior arrangement. Children welcome.

**ANY OTHER INFO** Lady Anne's Hotel is a Grade II-listed building set within3½ acres of formal gardens next to Burghley House. It got its name from Lady Anne Cecil, the 9th Earl of Exeter's sister. The house then belonged to Lord Rosslyn who established a stud farm and racing stables. The bar has cricketing theme which reflects the hotel owner, Geoff Hasting's, sporting love. Also civil wedding licence.

**HOW TO GET THERE** The hotel is just off A1 on B1081 on the outskirts of Stamford and the edge of Burghley Park.

The Brownlow Arms Country Hotel And Restaurant, Hough-on-the-Hill, Near Grantham, Lincolnshire NG32 2AZ
**Tel** 01400 250234 **Fax** 01400 250772
**Star ratings** Four crowns

**NO OF ROOMS** Seven.

**COST** From £52 per night bed and breakfast for a double room.

**SPECIAL BREAKS/OFFERS** Weekend Breaks: from £50 per person per night.

**FOOD** Traditional English with heavy emphasis on fresh, local produce. Beef Wellington is a typical example of its cuisine style. Extensive wine list. Award-winning real ales. Michelin award.

**SPORT ON OFFER/THAT CAN BE ARRANGED** Pheasant-shooting on local estates. Trout and carp fishing at local fisheries and Rutland Water. Hunting with the Belvoir and Quorn Foxhounds. Also go-karting, cycling and golf.

**SEASONS/BEST TIMES FOR SPECIALIST SPORTS** Traditional seasons.

**DOGS/CHILDREN WELCOME** Yes.

**ANY OTHER INFO** This 16th-century inn is run by Jayne and Gary Murphy. The house was originally the gamekeeper's cottage on Lord Brownlow's Belton estate. The pub hosts a meet for the Belvoir.

**HOW TO GET THERE** A1 north of Grantham. Turn right to Marston and Gelston. Hough-on-the-Hill is the next village.

The George Hotel, 71 St Martins, Stamford, Lincolnshire PE9 2LB
**Tel** 01780 750750 **Fax** 01780 750701
**e-mail** reservations@georgehotelofstamford.com **website** www.georgehotelofstamford.com
**Star ratings** ***AA

**NO OF ROOMS** 47.

**COST** From £78 per night bed and breakfast for a single room. From £103 per night bed and breakfast for a double room.

**SPECIAL BREAKS/OFFERS** From £109 per person dinner, bed and breakfast(minimum two-night weekend stay).

**FOOD** A la carte menu of traditional but imaginative English dishes served in oak-panelled dining-room. Informal meals available in the Garden Lounge. Extensive wine list. Recommended by Egon Ronay.

**SPORT ON OFFER/THAT CAN BE ARRANGED** Clay pigeon shooting locally. Fishing, sailing and bird-watching at Rutland Water. Foxhunting with the Cottesmore, Quorn, Belvoir and Woodland Pytchley Foxhounds. Riding and golf.

**SEASONS/BEST TIMES FOR SPECIALIST SPORTS** Traditional seasons.

**DOGS/CHILDREN WELCOME** Yes.

**ANY OTHER INFO** This coaching inn still retains much of its historical character. The London Room and York bar were once waiting rooms for the 40 coaches which stopped here each day. In the hallway hangs the picture of Daniel Lambert, the hotel's heaviest customer; he died in 1809 weighing 52 stone 11lb. Bedrooms have been individually designed by Julia Vannocci.

**HOW TO GET THERE** Off A1 at the roundabout signposted B1081 to Stamford. Follow road to the traffic lights and hotel is on the left at the lights.

The Red House Inn, Knipton, Grantham, Lincolnshire NG32 1RH
**Tel** 01476 870352 **Fax** 01476 870429

**NO OF ROOMS** Five.

**COST** From £28.50 per night bed and breakfast single occupancy. From £45 per night bed and breakfast for a double room.

**FOOD** Wide selection prepared using fresh local produce. Local game and fish in season are specialities. Comprehensive wine list.

**SPORT ON OFFER/THAT CAN BE ARRANGED** Hunting with the Belvoir and Quorn Foxhounds. Game-shooting on local estates. Fishing at Rutland Water. Golf locally.

**SEASONS/BEST TIMES FOR SPECIALIST SPORTS** Traditional seasons.

**DOGS/CHILDREN WELCOME** Yes, by prior appointment. Children welcome.

**ANY OTHER INFO** The Red House Inn is a former hunting lodge to Belvoir Castle which is just 1½ miles away. It has recently been taken over by Paul Lampier who was previously the manager. Very popular with the local sporting crowd.

**HOW TO GET THERE** Knipton is 1½ miles west of A607 midway between Grantham and Melton Mowbray.

Congham Hall Country House Hotel, Grimston, King's Lynn, Norfolk PE32 1AH
**Tel** 01485 600250 **Fax** 01485 601191
**e-mail** reception@conghamhallhotel.com
**Star ratings** ***AA Red/RAC Gold Ribbon Award

**NO OF ROOMS** 20.

**COST** From £130 per night bed and breakfast for a double/twin room.

**SPECIAL BREAKS/OFFERS** From £190 per person dinner, bed and breakfast for a two-night stay. Also themed weekends such as shooting and racing weekends.

**FOOD** Modern British with French Mediterranean influences. Fresh local produce used where possible. The herb garden provides fruit, vegetables and over 700 different varieties of herbs. Extensive wine list arranged by style, rather than country or region. Selection of malt whiskies and cognacs. Awarded two AA rosettes.

**SPORT ON OFFER/THAT CAN BE ARRANGED** Game-shooting on local estates. Clay pigeon shooting. Trout fishing on private lakes. Sea fishing, sailing, tennis, swimming and riding.

**SEASONS/BEST TIMES FOR SPECIALIST SPORTS** Traditional seasons.

**DOGS/CHILDREN WELCOME** No dogs allowed in hotel. Only children over seven-years-old.

**ANY OTHER INFO** Congham Hall is a Georgian manor house set within 30 acres of parkland, lawns and the renowned herb garden. It is furnished with antiques and fine art. Tennis court and swimming pool.

**HOW TO GET THERE** At the interchange of A47, A149 and A10 on the outskirts of King's Lynn follow A149 to the interchange with A148. Take A148 for 100yd and turn right to Congham Hall Herb Gardens. After about two miles the entrance to Congham Hall is on the left.

Strattons, 4 Ash Close, Swaffham, Norfolk PE37 7NH
**Tel** 01760 723845 **Fax** 01760 720458

**NO OF ROOMS** Seven.

**COST** From £70 per night bed and breakfast for a single room. From £90 per night bed and breakfast for a double room.

**SPECIAL BREAKS/OFFERS** Three nights for the price of two on a midweek break.

**FOOD** Modern English with the emphasis on local organic produce. Fresh herbs, flowers, fruit and vegetables – including wild berries and mushrooms – are gathered from the surrounding gardens and countryside; flour comes from the local mill. Well-stocked wine cellar. Four-course dinner £29.50 per person. Awarded County Restaurant of the Year 2000 from *The Good Food Guide*..

**SPORT ON OFFER/THAT CAN BE ARRANGED** Shooting on local estates such as Cockley Cley, Pickenham Hall and Bowes. Clay pigeon shooting, golf and riding.

**SEASONS/BEST TIMES FOR SEASONAL SPORTS** Traditional seasons.

**DOGS/CHILDREN WELCOME** Both welcome. Dogs (£5.50 per day) need to be cat tolerant. Children £15 extra if they stay in the same room.

**ANY OTHER INFO** Strattons, a Grade II Queen Anne house near the market place in Swaffham, is owned by Les and Vanessa Scott. The family's books and photos around the house add to the hotel's relaxed and friendly atmosphere. The hotel is a member of Green Globe and currently recycles, re-uses or composts most of its waste. Listed by *The Independent* as one of the top 50 hotels in Great Britain 1999.

**HOW TO GET THERE** The entrance to Ash Close is at the north end of the market place between William H Brown estate agents and Express Cleaners.

The Rose And Crown, Old Church Road, Snettisham, Norfolk PE31 7LX
**Tel** 01485 541382 **Fax** 01485 543172
**Star ratings** ****AA/English Tourist Board

**NO OF ROOMS** 11.

**COST** From £35 per person per night bed and breakfast for a double room.

**SPECIAL BREAKS/OFFERS** From £45 per person per night dinner, bed and breakfast for a midweek break (minimum two-night stay).

**FOOD** Lunch and evening menus based on fresh local produce, particularly fish, fruit and vegetables. This year's *Good Pub Guide* gives the hotel Good Food, Good Place to Stay and Good Wine by the Glass awards.

**SPORT ON OFFER/THAT CAN BE ARRANGED** Pheasant- and partridge-shooting locally. Sea fishing. Trout fishing in stocked lakes. Riding on the beach at Holme and Holkham. Also sailing, windsurfing, cycling, tennis and golf.

**SEASONS/BEST TIMES FOR SPECIALIST SPORTS** Traditional seasons.

**DOGS/CHILDREN WELCOME** Yes. Awarded the Lex Family Welcome gold award 1998.

**ANY OTHER INFO** Having recently completed a major programme of building and redecoration, Anthony and Jeannette Goodrich have managed to apply modern trends to this 14th-century inn without losing its original charm in the twisting passages, log fires and ancient beams. Also a walled garden.

**HOW TO GET THERE** In King's Lynn take A149 north to Cromer and Hunstanton. Stay on A419, despite all the roundabouts, until the right-hand turn to Snettisham. In the village take the first left turn into Old Church Road. The pub is 100yd on the left.

Tudor Gate Hotel, High Street, Finedon, Northamptonshire NN9 5JN
**Tel** 01933 680408 **Fax** 01933 680745
**e-mail** info@tudorgate-hotel.co.uk **website** www.tudorgate-hotel.co.uk
**Star ratings** **AA/English Tourist Board three crowns

**NO OF ROOMS** 27.

**COST** From £49 per night bed and breakfast for a single room. From £74 per night bed and breakfast for a double room.

**SPECIAL BREAKS/OFFERS** Please enquire. Members of the hotel's Silks Scene Club (£50 a year) receive 10 per cent discount on everything in the hotel. The bar is open exclusively to members every weekday between 5pm and 6pm and members also receive two free nights' accommodation in the first 12 months of club membership.

**FOOD** Both table d'hôte and à la carte menus. Fresh local produce used where possible. French baguettes and seafood a speciality. Racing theme in the bar. Extensive wine list. Real ales.

**SPORT ON OFFER/THAT CAN BE ARRANGED** Racing at Towcester and Newmarket. Golf locally.

**SEASONS/BEST TIMES FOR SPECIALIST SPORTS** Traditional seasons.

**DOGS/CHILDREN WELCOME** Yes.

**ANY OTHER INFO** Stuart and Gill Andrews own and run Tudor Gate Hotel, a 17th-century farm house. They are racing mad and own two racehorses which have not yet disgraced themselves. The hotel is sponsoring a race day at Newmarket in August.

**HOW TO GET THERE** M1 to Northampton. A45 to Wellingborough. Turn left to Finedon.

Otterburn Tower, Otterburn, Northumberland NE19 1NS
**Tel** 01830 520620 **Fax** 01830 521504
**e-mail** reservations@otterburntower.co.uk **website** www.otterburntower.co.uk
**Star ratings** ***AA

**NO OF ROOMS** 17.

**COST** From £55 per night bed and breakfast for a single room. From £70 per night bed and breakfast for a double room.

**SPECIAL BREAKS/OFFERS** Please enquire.

**FOOD** Menu based on fresh local produce – especially Northumberland beef and lamb. Extensive wine list.

**SPORT ON OFFER/THAT CAN BE ARRANGED** Pheasant-shooting on local farms and estates. Salmon, brown trout and sea-trout fishing on the hotel's own three-mile stretch of the River Reed. Also archery, clay pigeon shooting and falconry.

**SEASONS/BEST TIMES FOR SPECIALIST SPORTS** Traditional seasons.

**DOGS/CHILDREN WELCOME** Yes.

**ANY OTHER INFO** The Tower is a magnificent stone-walled fortress with shoulder-high ramparts and arrow-slit windows. It was built in 1076 as a defence against the Scots by a cousin of William the Conqueror. The hotel, fronted by formal gardens and surrounded by woodland, is owned by John Goodfellow who farms nearby and recently made the news as one of the first farmers to export beef to Europe since the ban was lifted.

**HOW TO GET THERE** From the A1: A1 to Newcastle, A696 to Otterburn. From the M6: M6 to Carlisle. A69 then A68 to Otterburn.

The Collingwood Arms Hotel, Cornhill-on-Tweed, Northumberland TD12 4UH
**Tel** 01890 882424 **Fax** 01890 883644
**Star ratings** **AA

**NO OF ROOMS** 16. One room has disabled facilities.

**COST** From £37.50 per night bed and breakfast for a single room. From £60 per night bed and breakfast for a double room.

**SPECIAL BREAKS/OFFERS** From £85 per person dinner, bed and breakfast in double/twin room for a two-night break.

**FOOD** A la carte and bar menus available in two restaurants. Sunday roast sirloin a speciality. Large selection of malt whiskies and real ales.

**SPORT THAT CAN BE ARRANGED** Salmon, brown and sea-trout fishing on Tweed and Till. Reservoir fishing for stocked trout. Also riding and golf.

**SEASONS/BEST TIMES FOR SPECIALIST SPORTS** Fishing: February to November.

**DOGS/CHILDREN WELCOME** Yes.

**ANY OTHER INFO** The hotel is a 300-year-old coaching inn, which offers old-fashioned hospitality close to Tweed.

**HOW TO GET THERE** On A697 between Edinburgh and Newcastle.

The Travellers Rest, Slaley, Hexham, Northumberland NE46 1TT
**Tel** 01434 673231 **Fax** 01434 673906
**e-mail** enq@travellersrest.sagehost.co.uk **website** www.travellersrest.sagesite.co.uk
**Star ratings** Four AA diamonds

**NO OF ROOMS** Three.

**COST** From £25 per person per night, bed and breakfast based on two people sharing a double room.

**FOOD** Large and varied menu. Extensive wine list. Four real ales.

**SPORT ON OFFER/THAT CAN BE ARRANGED** Pheasant-shooting on local estates. Clay pigeon shooting. Brown and rainbow trout fishing on Linnelwood Lake. Hunting with Tynedale Foxhounds. Golf locally.

**SEASONS/BEST TIMES FOR SPECIALIST SPORTS** Traditional seasons.

**DOGS/CHILDREN WELCOME** Yes.

**ANY OTHER INFO** This pub is managed by Jeremy and Lucy Irving who met while working at the nearby Slaley Hall Hotel. Jeremy looks after the front of the house and Lucy the kitchen. The house was built 300 years ago as a farmhouse but was converted to a pub at the beginning of last century. The Irvings host a meet once a year for the Tynedale Foxhounds.

**HOW TO GET THERE** M6, A69. Turn right to Hexham. Take B6306 out of Hexham and turn left to Slaley.

Tillmouth Park Country House Hotel, Cornhill-on-Tweed, Berwick upon Tweed, Northumberland TD12 4UU
**Tel** 01890 882255 **Fax** 01890 882540
**e-mail** reception@tillmouthpark.force9.co.uk **website** www.tillmouthpark.co.uk
**Star ratings** ***Silver Quality English Tourist Council

**NO OF ROOMS** 14.

**COST** From £65 per person per night bed and breakfast.

**SPECIAL BREAKS/OFFERS** From £83 per night dinner, bed and breakfast for two people sharing a twin/double room (minimum two-night stay) called the Border break. From 1 May to 31 August guests staying for three nights only pay for dinner on the third night.

**FOOD** Contemporary British food prepared by head chef Martin Furlong using fresh local produce. The restaurant offers a table d'hôte menu; the Bistro is more informal. Extensive wine list and a wide selection malt whiskies.

**SPORT ON OFFER/THAT CAN BE ARRANGED** Clay pigeon shooting on site. Pigeon-shooting on local farms. Mainly pheasant- and partridge-shooting on farms and estates between Duddo and Lauder. Brown trout, sea-trout and salmon fishing on Tweed and Till. Fishing on stocked lochs. Sea fishing off the Berwickshire coast. Roe stalking on various estates in the Alnwick area. Also golf and riding.

**SEASONS/BEST TIMES FOR SPECIALIST SPORTS** Traditional seasons.

**DOGS/CHILDREN WELCOME** Dogs, charged at £5 per night, are welcome in guest rooms but not public rooms. Children welcome. Up to 14-years-old charged £12.50 a night.

**ANY OTHER INFO** Tillmouth Park was built in 1882 by Charles Barry using stones from nearby Twizel Castle. This magnificent baronial country house is set in 15 acres of gardens. All bedrooms are furnished with antique and period furniture. The coast is only 15 miles away. Rod and drying rooms and a billiard room. Secure gun room.

**HOW TO GET THERE** From A1 (M) take A698 at East Ord roundabout. The hotel is about seven miles along on left after crossing the River Till.

The Inn For All Seasons, The Barringtons, Burford, Oxfordshire OX18 4TN
**Tel** 01451 844324 **Fax** 01451 844375
**e-mail** sharp@innforallseasons.com **website** www.innforallseasons.com
**Star ratings** ***AA

**NO OF ROOMS** 10.

**COST** From £42.50 per night bed and breakfast for a single room. From £85 per night bed and breakfast for a double room.

**SPECIAL BREAKS/OFFERS** From £59.50 per person per night dinner, bed and breakfast based on two people sharing a double room (minimum two-night stay).

**FOOD** French and European cuisine using fresh local products. Fish a speciality. About 50 bins on the wine list. Real ales, including the local Wychwood, and malt whiskies on offer. Awarded three AA rosettes.

**SPORT ON OFFER/THAT CAN BE ARRANGED** Pheasant- and partridge-shooting locally. Clay pigeon shooting. Fishing – please enquire. Hunting with the Heythrop and Vale of the White Horse Foxhounds. Also ballooning and golf.

**SEASONS/BEST TIMES FOR SPECIALIST SPORTS** Traditional seasons.

**DOGS/CHILDREN WELCOME** Yes.

**ANY OTHER INFO** The Sharpe family have owned this pub for 17 years and it is now run by their son Matthew and his wife Heather. It is a 16th-century coaching inn which has retained its character. Very popular during Cheltenham week. Egon Ronay and Johansens recommended.

**HOW TO GET THERE** Four miles west of Burford on A40 halfway between Cheltenham and Oxford.

King's Head Inn And Restaurant, Bledington, Near Kingham, Oxfordshire OX7 6XQ
**Tel** 01608 658365 **Fax** 01608 658902
**e-mail** kingshead@btinternet.com **website** btinternet.com/~kingshead
**Star ratings** ****AA/English Tourist Board

**NO OF ROOMS** 12.

**COST** From £45 per night bed and breakfast for a single room. From £65 per night bed and breakfast for a double/twin room.

**SPECIAL BREAKS/OFFERS** Please enquire.

**FOOD** Choose homemade food from the Snippets menu, Bar fare or the restaurant's à la carte menu. Cosmopolitan selection of wines introducing lesser known vineyards. Selection of real ales.

**SPORT THAT CAN BE ARRANGED** Shooting on local estates and farms. Trout fishing on a local lake. Clay pigeon shooting. Hunting with the Heythrop Foxhounds. Also quad biking and golf.

**SEASONS/BEST TIMES FOR SPECIALIST SPORTS** Traditional seasons.

**DOGS/CHILDREN WELCOME** No dogs. Children welcome.

**ANY OTHER INFO** The King's Head is a 15th-century inn which retains its original old beams, an inglenook fireplace and exposed stone walls. Prince Rupert of Rhine supposedly lodged here prior to the Battle of Stow in 1641. During the summer Morris dancers and musicians perform the Bledington Dances in the pub's courtyard. The traditional game of Aunt Sally takes place at the back of pub. Recommended by Johansens and Egon Ronay.

**HOW TO GET THERE** On B4450, four miles from Stow-on-the-Wold and six miles from Chipping Norton.

The Beetle And Wedge Hotel, Moulsford, Wallingford, Oxfordshire OX10 9JF
**Tel** 01491 651381 **Fax** 01491 651376

**NO OF ROOMS** 10.

**COST** From £90 to £120 per night bed and breakfast for a single room. From £135 to £150 per night bed and breakfast for a double room.

**SPECIAL BREAKS/OFFERS** From £195 per person dinner, bed and breakfast, champagne and flowers for a two-night stay.

**FOOD** Fresh local produce used where possible. Fine dining in the dining-room. Open charcoal fire in the Boathouse bar/restaurant where fresh fish and in-season game are grilled. Lunch served in the water garden. Puddings are a speciality. Extensive wine list. Mrs Smith, the hotel's owner, is a wine expert and eight of the staff are trained in wines. Awarded three AA rosettes.

**SPORT ON OFFER/THAT CAN BE ARRANGED** Coarse fishing on the River Thames. Shooting can be arranged through the Royal Berkshire Shooting School. Golf locally.

**SEASONS/BEST TIMES FOR SPECIALIST SPORTS** Traditional seasons.

**DOGS/CHILDREN WELCOME** Dogs in some rooms only. Children welcome.

**ANY OTHER INFO** The Beetle And Wedge Hotel lies on the banks of the River Thames. Its gardens run down to a stretch of the river immortalised in *The Wind In The Willows*. It was also here that Jerome K Jerome lived and chronicled the escapades of his friends' visits in *Three Men In A Boat*.

**HOW TO GET THERE** M40 to junction 6. Take B4009 to Watlington and then to Benson. Take A4074 to Reading for about a mile, go over the roundabout following A4130 to Reading for a mile. At roundabout take A329 direction for Didcot and Moulsford for a mile. At next roundabout turn left on A329 to Pangbourne and Moulsford. In Moulsford take a left into Ferry Lane. Or take M4 to junction 12. Take A4 to Newbury then A340 to Pangbourne. At Pangbourne take A329 to Goring and Wallingford. In Moulsford turn right at the crossroads into Ferry Lane.

The Lamb Inn, Sheep Street, Burford, Oxfordshire OX18 4LR
**Tel** 01993 823155 **Fax** 01993 822228
**Star ratings** ***AA

**NO OF ROOMS** 15.

**COST** From £100 to £120 per night bed and breakfast for a double room.

**SPECIAL BREAKS/OFFERS** Please enquire.

**FOOD** Fresh local produce used where possible. Extensive wine list. Awarded two AA rosettes.

**SPORT ON OFFER/THAT CAN BE ARRANGED** Hunting with Heythrop and Vale of White Horse Foxhounds. Shooting locally. Fishing on the River Windrush and at Lechlade. Golf locally.

**SEASONS/BEST TIMES FOR SPECIALIST SPORTS** Traditional seasons.

**DOGS/CHILDREN WELCOME** Dogs charged at £5 a night. Children welcome.

**ANY OTHER INFO** The Lamb has been an inn for 500 years. Sheep Street used to be the main thoroughfare for Burford and it was therefore very popular with travellers and drovers alike. It also acted as the dormy house for the neighbouring priory. Caroline and Richard de Wolf have owned this pub for 18 years. Johansens recommended.

**HOW TO GET THERE** Turn off A40 for Burford on to A361 to Chipping Norton. In Burford, Sheep Street is on the left of the High Street.

The Stonor Arms Hotel, Stonor, Near Henley-on-Thames, Oxfordshire RG9 6HE
**Tel** 01491 638866 **Fax** 01491 638863
**e-mail** stonorarms.hotel@virgin.net **website** www.stonor-arms.co.uk
**Star ratings** ***AA

**NO OF ROOMS** 10. Ground-floor bedrooms available with doors on to the garden.

**COST** From £99 per night bed and breakfast for a single room. From £125 per night bed and breakfast for a double room.

**SPECIAL BREAKS/OFFERS** Midweek break: from £125 dinner, bed and breakfast based on two people sharing a double room (minimum two-night stay). Weekend break: from £145 dinner, bed and breakfast based on two people sharing a double room (minimum two-night stay).

**FOOD** Modern English. Adventurous seasonal menu. Bar decorated with historic rowing memorabilia. Bar meals available. Creative wine list. Local beers served. Awarded two AA rosettes.

**SPORT THAT CAN BE ARRANGED** Game-shooting locally. Coarse fishing on the River Thames. Also riding, golf and boating.

**SEASONS/BEST TIMES FOR SPECIALIST SPORTS** Traditional seasons.

**DOGS/CHILDREN WELCOME** Yes.

**ANY OTHER INFO** The Stonor Arms is a privately owned country-house hotel. Walled garden. All bedrooms have been individually decorated and furnished with English and French antiques. Own licence for civil weddings.

**HOW TO GET THERE** Take A4130 out of Henley. Turn left on to B480 to Assendons and Stonor. The hotel is on the right after about three miles.

Ailean Chraggan Hotel, Weem, By Aberfeldy, Perthshire PH15 2LD
**Tel** 01887 820346 **Fax** 01887 829009
**e-mail** aileanchraggan@btconnect.com
**Star rating** ***Scottish Tourist Board

**NO OF ROOMS** Five.

**COST** From £38.50 per person per night bed and breakfast for a double room based on two people sharing.

**SPECIAL BREAKS/OFFERS** Rate reduced to £33.50 per person per night for a five-night stay or more.

**FOOD** Menu changes daily with strong emphasis on seafood and game in season. Local ingredients used wherever possible. Over 100 single malt whiskies stocked as well as 55 bins offered on the wine list.

**SPORT ON OFFER/THAT CAN BE ARRANGED** Salmon and brown trout fishing on the River Tay. Roe and red deer stalking on local estates. Grouse- and pheasant-shooting and wildfowling on local estates. Also golf, tennis, watersports and pony trekking.

**SEASONS/BEST TIMES FOR SPECIALIST SPORTS** Salmon: May and June.

**DOGS/CHILDREN WELCOME** Yes.

**ANY OTHER INFO** The hotel has been owned by the Gillespie family since it was started in 1963. It is set within its own two acres and looks south over the River Tay. Ailean Chraggan is renowned for its hospitality and sporting emphasis as Alistair Gillespie is a keen fisherman.

**HOW TO GET THERE** Weem is north of Glasgow and Edinburgh on A9. From there take A827 to Aberfeldy. At Aberfeldy turn left on to B846 and then right to the hotel.

Altnaharra Hotel, Altnaharra, By Lairg, Sutherland IV27 4UE
**Tel** & **Fax** 01549 411222
**e-mail** altnaharra@btinternet.com **website** www.altnaharra.com

**NO OF ROOMS** 15.

**COST** From £59 per person per night dinner, bed and breakfast for a single room. From £69 per person per night dinner, bed and breakfast for a double room.

**SPECIAL BREAKS/OFFERS** Fisherman's week: from £345 per person March and April; from £445 per person 1 to 22 May. Includes seven nights' dinner, bed and breakfast, packed lunch and fishing on Loch Naver, River Mudale, Loch Hope and trout lochs.

**FOOD** Traditional Scottish fare with a Continental touch. Game, venison and lamb come from neighbouring estates. Beef and pork from organic farms in Forres. Seafood is delivered daily and salmon, trout, sea-trout and char are caught in the hotel's own waters. Extensive wine list with a wide choice of vintages and varieties.

**SPORT ON OFFER/THAT CAN BE ARRANGED** Salmon, sea-trout and brown trout fishing on Lochs Naver and Hope. Wild brown trout fishing on Lochs Plantation, Meadie, Loyal, Hakel, Craggie, Staink, Breac Buidhe, Eileanach, Halium and Na Bieste. The hotel's beat on the River Mudale produces both salmon and brown trout – as does the River Strathmore. Days can be booked on the Rivers Borgie, Naver and Shin. Gillies available for £35 per day. Fly-fishing tuition charged at £80 per day. Also stalking, woodcock-shooting, clay pigeon shooting and golf.

**SEASONS/BEST TIMES FOR SPECIALIST SPORTS** Fishing: March to the end of September.

**DOGS/CHILDREN WELCOME** Yes.

**ANY OTHER INFO** Anne Nielsen has owned and managed Altnaharra since 1994. It is one of the oldest sporting hotels in Scotland. Fly-fishing courses cost £1,180 per person for six days and £690 for three days. This includes fishing, gillies, dinner, bed and breakfast, packed lunches, tackle hire and tuition.

**HOW TO GET THERE** From Inverness take A9 to Wick. At Bonar Bridge turn left for Lairg on A836 and follow signs for Tongue.

Ardanaiseig Hotel, Kilchrenan by Taynuilt, Argyll PA35 1HE
**Tel** 01866 833333 **Fax** 01866 833222
**e-mail** ardanaiseig@clara.net **website** www.ardanaiseig-hotel.com
**Star ratings** ****Scottish Tourist Board

**NO OF ROOMS** 16.

**COST** From £78 to £120 per person per night bed and breakfast based on two people sharing a double room. Single supplement £30.

**SPECIAL BREAKS/OFFERS** Spring and autumn special three-day breaks. Summer Treats rate for last-minute bookings.

**FOOD** Modern Scottish/French cuisine. Imaginative use of fresh produce – seafood a speciality. Extensive wine list. Over 50 malt whiskies on offer. Previously awarded three AA rosettes and new chef set to achieve similar status in the near future.

**SPORT ON OFFER/THAT CAN BE ARRANGED** Salmon and sea-trout fishing on the River Awe. Wild brown and rainbow trout, pike, char and perch fishing on Loch Awe. Boats hired for £35 a day (engine) or £25 a day (rowing). Gillies charged at £35 a day or £12 an hour. Trout fishing on the hotel's own pond. Fishing on Inverawe Fisheries. Deep sea fishing. Clay pigeon shooting. Also golf, riding, cycling, tennis and sailing.

**SEASONS/BEST TIMES FOR SPECIALIST SPORTS** Brown and rainbow trout: 15 March to 6 October.

**DOGS/CHILDREN WELCOME** Yes.

**ANY OTHER INFO** Ardanaiseig, designed by William Burn for Colonel Archibald Campbell in 1834, is an old country house overlooking the mysterious islands and crannogs (lake dwellings) of Loch Awe – the longest loch in Britain. It is set within wooded gardens which house one of Argyll's best collections of rhododendrons and azaleas, as well as specimen trees originating from the foothills of the Himalayas and a 19th-century walled garden providing herbs for the kitchen. The house is furnished with antiques, works of art and fresh flowers. Tennis court, billiards room and boat house. Annual midsummer festival of art and music. Plans afoot for the 100-acre estate to be used as an outdoor setting for regular exhibitions of sculpture inspired by nature and Celtic legend.

**HOW TO GET THERE** From Glasgow or Oban: A85 to the junction with B845. Follow to Kilchrenan. At the pub turn left along a three-mile single track to the hotel.

Atholl Palace Hotel, Pitlochry, Perthshire PH16 5LY
**Tel** 01796 472400 **Fax** 01796 473036
**Star ratings** ***AA

**NO OF ROOMS** 76.

**COST** From £55 to £75 per person dinner, bed and breakfast based on two people sharing a double room.

**SPECIAL BREAKS/OFFERS** Two-night breaks from £94 per person dinner, bed and breakfast based on two people sharing a double room.

**FOOD** Traditional Scottish fare using fresh local produce. Game a speciality. Comprehensive wine list. Good selection malt whiskies.

**SPORT ON OFFER/THAT CAN BE ARRANGED** Salmon, sea-trout, brown trout and coarse fishing on the Rivers Tay and Tummel. Pheasant-shooting on local estates.

**SEASONS/BEST TIMES FOR SPECIALIST SPORTS** Traditional seasons.

**DOGS/CHILDREN WELCOME** Yes.

**ANY OTHER INFO** Atholl Palace is a fine example of Scottish baronial. Although it may look like a castle it was in fact built 120 years ago as a hotel. It is set above 48 acres of wooded parkland.

**HOW TO GET THERE** From Edinburgh M90 to Perth. A9 to Inverness. From Pitlochry exit, turn right immediately following the railway bridge on the way into town.

Auchterarder House, Auchterarder, Perthshire PH3 1DZ
**Tel** 01764 663646 **Fax** 01764 662939
**e-mail** auchterarder@wrensgroup.com **website** www.auchterarder.com
**Star ratings** ***AA/****Scottish Tourist Board

**NO OF ROOMS** 15.

**COST** From £125 per night bed and breakfast for a single room. From £195 per night bed and breakfast for a double room.

**SPECIAL BREAKS/OFFERS** Please enquire.

**FOOD** Victorian dining-room with splendid cuisine from former Scottish Chef of the Year, Willie Deans. The original cellars carry 400 wines. Awarded two AA rosettes.

**SPORT THAT CAN BE ARRANGED** Pheasant-, grouse- and partridge-shooting on local estates. Stalking on local estates. Fishing on the River Tay. Also golf.

**SEASONS/BEST TIMES FOR SPECIALIST SPORTS** Traditional seasons.

**DOGS/CHILDREN WELCOME** Dogs welcome with own bedding. No children under 12-years-old.

**ANY OTHER INFO** Auchterarder is an opulent hotel set in its own 17 acres of grounds and boasts over 400 different species of rhododendron.

**HOW TO GET THERE** Ten miles south of Perth on A9. Go into the village of Auchterarder on A824. Turn right on to B8062 (signposted Crieff). Auchterarder House is 1½ miles on the right.

Balbirnie House Hotel, Markinch, By Glenrothes, Fife KY7 6NE
**Tel** 01592 610066 **Fax** 01592 610529
**e-mail** balbirnie@breathemail.net **website** www.balbirnie.co.uk
**Star ratings** ****AA Red

**NO OF ROOMS** 30.

**COST** From £125 per night bed and breakfast for a single room. From £185 per night bed and breakfast for a double room.

**SPECIAL BREAKS/OFFERS** From £89.50 per person per night bed and breakfast on a Weekend Pampered Break (minimum two-night stay). From £115 per person per night bed and breakfast on a Golfing Enthusiast Break (minimum two-night stay). Please enquire for details of other breaks.

**FOOD** Scottish cooking using seasonal fresh local produce. The Old Library Bar is well stocked with a fine range of ports, brandies and 110 malt whiskies. Balbirnie's wine list features over 250 wines from around the world. Awarded two AA rosettes. Member of Taste of Scotland.

**SPORT ON OFFER/THAT CAN BE ARRANGED** Salmon and trout fishing on the River Tay. Local game-shooting. Also falconry, clay pigeon shooting, off-road driving, motoracing, tennis and riding. There's golf within Balbirnie Park. Awarded 1998 Golf International Hotel of the Year.

**SEASONS/BEST TIMES FOR SPECIALIST SPORTS** Traditional seasons, otherwise all year.

**DOGS/CHILDREN WELCOME** Yes.

**ANY OTHER INFO** Balbirnie is a unique multi-award winning hotel which combines understated luxury with superb service and outstanding value. It is a delightful old house, Grade A listed and sits as the centrepiece of a beautiful 400-acre country estate.

**HOW TO GET THERE** From Edinburgh follow the signs for Forth Road Bridge/M90. Turn off on to A92/Glenrothes road, cross three roundabouts, following Tay Bridge signs. Turn right at Balbirnie Park/Markinch signs.

Blairmore House, Glass, Huntly, Aberdeenshire AB5 4XH
**Tel** 01466 700200 **Fax** 01466 700205
**website** www.blairmorehouse

**NO OF ROOMS** Nine.

**COST** The house is let on an all-inclusive basis at £1,500 plus VAT per night for a minimum of two nights.

**FOOD** Dinners, ranging from gourmet dinners to Scottish evenings, are cooked by chefs of the Scottish Culinary Team. There is a strong emphasis on local produce especially beef, lamb, game and salmon. Fruit and vegetables are sourced from Blairmore's own garden during the summer. Extensive wine list and a good range of malt whiskies.

**SPORT THAT CAN BE ARRANGED** Driven- and walked-up pheasant-shooting from estates such as Drummuir, Bognie, Haddo and Aswanley. Roe and red deer stalking from Mar Lodge and Aswanley. Partridge- and duck-shooting at Haddo and Aswanley. Also wildfowling and clay pigeon shooting. Salmon and sea-trout fishing on the Rivers Spey and Deveron. Golf.

**SEASONS/BEST TIMES FOR SPECIALIST SPORTS** Shooting: October to January. Red deer stalking: September and October. Roe deer stalking: May to August.

**DOGS/CHILDREN WELCOME** Blairmore House is not suitable for dogs or children but comfortable accommodation can be arranged in three cottages on the estate.

**ANY OTHER INFO** Blairmore House, originally built for the Scottish entrepreneur Alexander Geddes (the grain king of Chicago) and now owned by Hans and Monique Baumann, is set a within 40-acre wooded estate. Prior to the Baumanns moving to Blairmore the house was a prep school. The bedrooms have retained their dormitory names. Monique organises flower arranging and cookery courses for the ladies while the men are out shooting or fishing by day. There are also facilities for sauna, massages and beauty treatments as well as shopping and sightseeing outings. Three further cottages available for let.

**HOW TO GET THERE** Follow A96 through Huntly towards Inverness. Take A920 to Dufftown for about five miles. At the signpost to Blairmore School turn left and follow the road to Blairmore House.

Buccleuch Arms Hotel, The Green, St Boswells, Melrose, Roxburghshire TD6 0EW
**Tel** 01835 822243 **Fax** 01835 823965
**e-mail** bucchotel@aol.com **website** www.buccleucharms.com
**Star ratings** **AA/***Scottish Tourist Board

**NO OF ROOMS** 20.

**COST** From £42 per night bed and breakfast for a single room. From £75 per night bed and breakfast for a double room.

**SPECIAL BREAKS/OFFERS** From £45 per person dinner, bed and breakfast (minimum two-night stay). Winter breaks from £39 per person dinner, bed and breakfast. Other seasonal offers available.

**FOOD** Fresh local produce used to combine the best of French and Scottish cuisine. Garden restaurant recommended by Taste Of Scotland. Fine selection of beers and wines.

**SPORT ON OFFER/THAT CAN BE ARRANGED** Trout fishing both on Tweed and stocked lochs. Driven and rough pheasant- and partridge-shooting. Goose-shooting. Foxhunting with the Buccleuch, Berwickshire, Lauderdale and Jedforest. Golf, cycling, pony trekking and tennis.

**SEASONS/BEST TIMES FOR SPECIALIST SPORTS** Traditional seasons.

**DOGS/CHILDREN WELCOME** Yes.

**ANY OTHER INFO** This well-known 16th-century family-run coaching inn is regularly frequented by locals eating in the restaurant. Sporting prints on the wall reflect where this hotel's interests lie.

**HOW TO GET THERE** Roadside location on A68, 65 miles from Newcastle or 35 miles south of Edinburgh.

Burts Hotel, Market Square, Melrose TD6 9PL
**Tel** 01896 822285 **Fax** 01896 822870
**e-mail** burtshotel@aol.com **website** www.burtshotel.co.uk
**Star ratings** ***AA/****Scottish Tourist Board

**NO OF ROOMS** 20.

**COST** From £50 per night bed and breakfast for a single room. From £88 per night bed and breakfast for a double/twin room.

**SPECIAL BREAKS/OFFERS** From £70 per night dinner, bed and breakfast for a single room or £65 per person per night for a double/twin room, dinner, bed and breakfast (minimum two-night stay). Special shooting packages for dinner, bed and breakfast. Out-of-season special package available; information on request.

**FOOD** Choose from either table d'hôte or à la carte menus: lunch £20.75; dinner £27.75. Bar meals available at lunch and in the evenings. Extensive wine list. Real ales and over 60 malt whiskies on offer. Beef is sourced from quality assured farms as the hotel is a member of the Scotch Beef Club. Restaurant awarded two AA rosettes. Members of Taste of Scotland.

**SPORT THAT CAN BE ARRANGED** Salmon fishing on Tweed. Driven pheasant-shooting on Buccleuch, Lothian and Mertoun estates. Wildfowling locally. Golf, cycling and pony trekking.

**SEASONS/BEST TIMES FOR SPECIALIST SPORTS** Fishing: either February to June or September to November. Shooting: from October to January.

**DOGS/CHILDREN WELCOME** Yes.

**ANY OTHER INFO** Burts, adorned with hunting and shooting prints and fishing rods hanging from the ceiling, will make all sporting enthusiasts feel at home. The hotel has been run by the Henderson family for over 25 years. Rugby sevens was invented in Melrose on 28 April 1883, and the Melrose annual event is still one of the largest and most prestigious days in the rugby calendar.

**HOW TO GET THERE** On A6091, two miles from A68. Burts Hotel is 38 miles south of Edinburgh.

Corrour House Hotel, Rothiemurchus, By Aviemore, Inverness-shire, PH22 1QH
**Tel** 01479 810220 **Fax** 01479 811500
**website** www.corrourhouse.co.uk
**Star rating** ****Scottish Tourist Board

**NO OF ROOMS** Eight.

**COST** From £60 per person per night dinner, bed and breakfast based on two people sharing in a double room.

**SPECIAL BREAKS/OFFERS** Weekly rates available.

**FOOD** Traditional four-course Scottish dinners prepared using fresh local produce including herbs and vegetables from the hotel's garden. Picnic and shoot lunches available. Taste of Scotland commendation. Over 100 bins of wine stocked, as well as a good range of malt whiskies – especially Speyside malts.

**SPORT THAT CAN BE ARRANGED** Roe buck, stag and hind stalking. Driven pheasant- and rough days to teams of guns. Trout and salmon fishing on the River Spey. All sport arranged on local estates.

**SEASONS/BEST TIMES FOR SPECIALIST SPORTS** Roe buck: May, June and July; stags: September and October; hinds: November. Driven- and rough-shooting between November and January; fishing between April and September.

**DOGS/CHILDREN WELCOME** Yes.

**ANY OTHER INFO** Corrour House was originally built in the Victorian era as a dower house by the Grants of Rothiemurchus estate. Now the hotel is run by David and Sheana Catto and their family. It is set in four acres of secluded gardens with views to the Cairngorms. The whole house can be reserved for shooting parties. Recommended by Johansens and Michelin.

**HOW TO GET THERE** Half a mile from Aviemore on B970. Follow signs for Rothiemurchus and Coylumbridge.

Dunain Park Hotel, Dunain, Inverness IV3 8JN
**Tel** 01463 230512 **Fax** 01463 224532
**e-mail** dunainparkhotel@btinternet.com **website** www.dunainparkhotel.co.uk
**Star ratings** ****Scottish Tourist Board

**NO OF ROOMS** 13.

**COST** From £138 to £198 per night bed and breakfast for a double/twin room based on two people sharing.

**SPECIAL BREAKS/OFFERS** Three-day Christmas and New Year breaks. Low season dinner, bed and breakfast rates from October to April.

**FOOD** Modern Scottish with a French influence. Salmon, scallops, venison, beef and lamb all bought locally. Ann Nicoll is a Master Chef of Great Britain. Herbs, soft fruit and vegetables are grown within the hotel's two-acre walled garden. Home-baked bread and homemade preserves. Extensive wine list and over 200 malt whiskies on offer.

**SPORT ON OFFER/THAT CAN BE ARRANGED** Salmon fishing on the River Ness. Stocked brown trout in Loch Tarvie. Pheasant-shooting and stalking on local estates. Also swimming, riding and golf.

**SEASONS/BEST TIMES FOR SPECIALIST SPORTS** Traditional seasons.

**DOGS/CHILDREN WELCOME** Dogs welcome by arrangement. Well-behaved children welcome.

**ANY OTHER INFO** Dunain Park is a Georgian country house set in six acres of garden and woodlands, owned and run by Edward and Ann Nicoll for 14 years. Originally it was a shooting lodge built by the Duke of Gordon. During the Battle of Culloden it was taken from him by the Hanoverians as he was one of Bonnie Prince Charlie's supporters. The hotel has an indoor heated swimming pool and a sauna situated in a log cabin on the grounds. Two cottages to let. Drying room.

**HOW TO GET THERE** A mile outside Inverness on A82 to Fort William.

Dunans Castle, Glendaruel, Argyll PA22 3AD
**Tel** and **Fax** 01369 820380
**e-mail** marr@dunans-castle.co.uk **website** www.dunans-castle.co.uk
**Star ratings** *****AA

**NO OF ROOMS** Six clan-named suites each with a four-poster bed and en-suite Victorian bathroom.

**COST** From £75 to £105 per suite per night bed and breakfast.

**SPECIAL BREAKS/OFFERS** Fishing and shooting weekends on application.

**FOOD** Traditional Scottish fare all prepared by the Lady of Marr using fresh local produce. Wine complimentary. Five-course dinner is £17.50.

**SPORT ON OFFER/THAT CAN BE ARRANGED** Clay pigeon shooting and archery on site. Complimentary salmon fishing for guests on the River Ruel, the second largest yielding salmon river. Shooting, stalking and watersports can be arranged locally. Cycling and golf nearby.

**SEASONS/BEST TIMES FOR SPECIALIST SPORTS** Traditional seasons, otherwise all year round.

**DOGS/CHILDREN WELCOME** Yes.

**ANY OTHER INFO** Dunans is a Franco-Scots baronial listed castle, the private home of the Lord and Lady of Marr. The sole means of entering the castle is across a 60ft ravine over an A-listed bridge. Once there, guests receive exceptional value for money which is all down to the Lady of Marr's love of entertaining. In her own words: "It's our home and if we could do it for free we would." Dunans boasts its own private chapel which is available for weddings. In the grounds is a Douglas fir standing at 213ft 6in making it the UK's tallest tree. The estate is also well known for its exceptional flora and fauna.

**HOW TO GET THERE** Directions are complicated. Arrange for the castle to fax or send instructions.

Farleyer House Hotel, Aberfeldy, Perthshire PH15 2JE
**Tel** 01887 820332 **Fax** 01887 829430
**e-mail** reservations@farleyer.com **website** www.farleyer.com
**star ratings** ****AA

**NO OF ROOMS** 19.

**COST** From £45 per person per night bed and breakfast based on two people sharing a double room.

**FOOD** Traditional Scottish fare using fresh local produce where possible. Extensive wine list. Selection of malt whiskies. Member of Taste of Scotland. Recommended by *The Good Food Guide* and Michelin.

**SPORT ON OFFER/THAT CAN BE ARRANGED** Salmon fishing on three beats of the River Tay. Red and roe deer stalking on local estates. Driven- and walked-up pheasant-shooting on local estates.

**SEASONS/BEST TIMES FOR SPECIALIST SPORTS** Salmon: June, September and October.

**DOGS/CHILDREN WELCOME** Dogs only in outside facilities. Children welcome.

**ANY OTHER INFO** Farleyer was originally the dower house to the Menzies family. It then became the shooting lodge and eventually a hotel. It is currently owned by Derek Reed. The hotel is richly and individually decorated with antiques and works of art.There are 45 acres of landscaped gardens surrounding the house.

**HOW TO GET THERE FROM** A9 follow signs for Aberfeldy then take B846 towards Kinloch Rannoch out of Aberfeldy to the hotel.

Four Seasons Hotel, St Fillans, Perthshire PH6 2NF
**Tel** 01764 685333 **Fax** 01764 685444
**e-mail** info@thefourseasonshotel.co.uk **website** www.thefourseasonshotel.co.uk
**Star ratings** ***AA

**NO OF ROOMS** 18.

**COST** From £32 to £44 per person per night bed and breakfast. From £53 to £65 per person per night dinner, bed and breakfast.

**SPECIAL BREAKS/OFFERS** Please enquire.

**FOOD** Contemporary Scottish cuisine using the best available local produce to cater for both the traditional and adventurous dishes. Two restaurants. Large selection wines and malt whiskies. Member of Taste of Scotland. Awarded two AA rosettes.

**SPORT ON OFFER/THAT CAN BE ARRANGED** Brown trout, sea-trout and salmon fishing on Rivers Tay and Earn. Brown and rainbow trout fishing in Loch Earn. Stalking and shooting can all be arranged locally. Waterskiing, sailing and white-water rafting on Loch Earn. Off-road driving, go-kart racing, archery, cycling and golf.

**SEASONS/BEST TIMES FOR SPECIALIST SPORTS** Traditional seasons.

**DOGS/CHILDREN WELCOME** Dogs welcome. Children under three-years-old are free of charge. Three- to 11-year olds are charged half room price.

**ANY OTHER INFO** Loch Earn is six miles long and lies in the very heart of Scotland. The Four Seasons Hotel occupies one of the finest lochside settings in the Highlands and is an ideal setting for a family holiday. Six chalets are available for let behind the hotel. Egon Ronay and *Which?* guide recommended. Open March to Hogmanay.

**HOW TO GET THERE** On A85 at the west of St Fillans.

Glenapp Castle, Ballantrae, Ayrshire KA26 0NZ
**Tel** 01465 831212 **Fax** 01465 831000
**e-mail** castle@glenapp.demon.co.uk **website** www.glenappcastle.com

**NO OF ROOMS** 17. Disabled facilities.

**COST** From £410 to £500 per couple per night including all meals, house wines and spirits.

**FOOD** The French chef uses fresh local produce. Extensive Connoisseurs wine list. Selection local malt whiskies and other malts.

**SPORT ON OFFER/THAT CAN BE ARRANGED** Pheasant- and grouse-shooting on Glenapp and other local estates. Stalking on local estates. Salmon fishing on the Rivers Stinchar and Cree. Golf on local championship course. Curling.

**SEASONS/BEST TIMES FOR SPECIALIST SPORTS** Curling: April to October, otherwise traditional seasons.

**DOGS/CHILDREN WELCOME** Yes. Dogs only allowed in ground-floor bedrooms. Children aged five- to 15-years-old charged at £100 per day.

**ANY OTHER INFO** Glenapp Castle was built in 1870 by David Bryce for James Hunter, Ayshire's Deputy Lord Lieutenant. The castle was then bought by the Earl of Inchcape in 1917. It stayed with this family until 1982 when it was bought by the McMillans in 1994. The McMillans' daughter and son-in-law, Fay and Graham Cowan, have spent the past 5½ years restoring the grounds and redecorating the castle which they have furnished with antiques and original art. There are 30 acres of gardens and woodland including a walled garden and a 150ft Victorian glasshouse. The atmosphere is redolent of a country-house party. Admission to the castle and grounds is only possible for those with a prior reservation. The hotel is open from April to October.

**HOW TO GET THERE** Glenapp Castle is a mile from A77 Glasgow to Stranraer road near the village of Ballantrae.

Kinloch House Hotel, By Blairgowrie, Perthshire PH10 6SG
**Tel** 01250 884237 **Fax** 01250 884333
**e-mail** info@kinlochhouse.com **website** www.kinlochhouse.com
**Star ratings** ***AA Red/*****Scottish Tourist Board

**NO OF ROOMS** 20. Disabled facilities.

**COST** From £101 per night dinner, bed and breakfast for a single room. From £211.50 per night dinner, bed and breakfast for a double room.

**SPECIAL BREAKS/OFFERS** Shooting breaks available from November to 18 December. Cookery workshops. Please enquire.

**FOOD** Extensive daily changing menu using the finest Scottish produce and organic ingredients from the hotel's own walled garden. Over 300 wines on offer. Awarded three AA rosettes.

**SPORT ON OFFER/THAT CAN BE ARRANGED** Pheasant-, partridge-, grouse-shooting (driven or walked-up) from £150 per gun, excluding hotel accommodation. Also wildfowling. Salmon and trout fishing on lochs or the River Tay. Rod room. Sailing boat available to experienced sailors. The hotel has a swimming pool, sauna, steam room, spa, multigym and masseuse. Also golf, riding, cycling and falconry.

**SEASONS/BEST TIMES FOR SPECIALIST SPORTS** Shooting from November to December, falconry all year and fishing in the spring.

**DOGS/CHILDREN WELCOME** Dogs welcome in certain rooms. Children of all ages welcome, but only seven-year-olds and over allowed in the dining-room.

**ANY OTHER INFO** Kinloch House is set in 25 acres of wood and parkland with views over Marlee Loch to the Sidlaw Hills beyond. This country house with oak-panelled halls and first floor galleries has been run by owners David and Sarah Shentall since 1981 and is well known for its warm welcome. Johansens recommended.

**HOW TO GET THERE** Three miles west of Blairgowrie on A923 to Dunkeld or eight miles east of Dunkeld from A9 to Blairgowrie.

Kinnaird, Kinnaird estate, By Dunkeld, Perthshire PH8 0LB
**Tel** 01796 482440 **Fax** 01796 482289
**e-mail** enquiry@kinnairdestate.com **website** www.kinnairdestate.com
**Star ratings** ***AA Red

**NO OF ROOMS** Nine rooms and a further nine cottages.

**COST** From £345 to £440 dinner, bed and breakfast per room per night based on two people sharing.

**SPECIAL BREAKS/OFFERS** Winter rates: from £225 dinner, bed and breakfast per room per night (minimum two-night stay).

**FOOD** Both a restaurant (with hand-painted Italian frescoes) and private dining-room. Only finest quality produce used. Well-stocked wine cellar. Extensive list of aperitifs and traditional malt whiskies. Awarded an RAC gold ribbon and two AA rosettes.

**SPORT ON OFFER** Salmon fishing on five miles of the River Tay. Wild brown trout fishing in three hill lochs within the estate. Pheasant-, duck-, partridge-, limited grouse-, pigeon- and rabbit-shooting within the estate. Tennis court on site. Also croquet, bowls and clay pigeon shooting. Golf and riding nearby.

**SEASONS/BEST TIMES FOR SPECIALIST SPORTS** Traditional seasons.

**DOGS/CHILDREN WELCOME** No dogs in Kinnaird but heated kennels available on the estate. No under 12-year-olds in the hotel but welcome in the cottages.

**ANY OTHER INFO** Kinnaird, an Edwardian mansion, is set within its own 9,000-acre estate. Constance Ward, the owner, has furnished the house with fine antiques, china and works of art. Within the house there are a number of cases displaying fine salmon caught by the family on Kinnaird's beat.

**HOW TO GET THERE** From the south: from Perth take A9. After 15 miles reach Dunkeld. Do not exit but continue another two miles. Turn left on to B898 signed to Dalguise, Kinnaird and Balnaguard. From the north: from Pitlochry follow A9 to Ballinluig. Continue towards Dunkeld. Five miles south of Ballinluig turn right after crossing the River Tay on to B898 to Dalguise, Kinnaird and Balnaguard. Kinnaird is on the right after 4½ miles.

Knockomie Hotel, Grantown Road, Forres, Moray IV36 2SG
**Tel** 01309 673146 **Fax** 01309 673290
**e-mail** stay@knockomie.co.uk **website** www.knockomie.co.uk
**Star ratings** ****Scottish Tourist Board

**NO OF ROOMS** 15.

**COST** From £75 per night bed and breakfast for a single room. From £90 per night bed and breakfast for a double/twin room.

**SPECIAL BREAKS/OFFERS** From £99 per person per night dinner, bed and breakfast during September and October (minimum two-night stay).

**FOOD** Traditional Scottish fare with a Continental twist. Seafood, beef and vegetables all sourced locally. Member of the Scottish Beef Club. Awarded two red AA rosettes. Members of Taste of Scotland.

**SPORT ON OFFER/THAT CAN BE ARRANGED** Salmon and sea-trout and grilse fishing on the River Findhorn. Wild brown trout fishing on local lochs. Stocked rainbow trout fishing in stocked lochs. Grouse-shooting on Knockando estate. Stalking on Dallas estate. Pheasant-, partridge-, pigeon- and rabbit-shooting on local estates. Also golf.

**SEASONS/BEST TIMES FOR SPECIALIST SPORTS** Fishing: March to September. Golf: March to October. Shooting: traditional seasons.

**DOGS/CHILDREN WELCOME** Yes.

**ANY OTHER INFO** Knockomie was built about 120 years ago for the Fraser family when they returned from the Indian tea plantations. It was redesigned in the Arts and Crafts style in 1914 and remains one of the best examples of this style in the north of Scotland. The house, which overlooks the Royal Burgh of Forres and is set within 11 acres of gardens, and is now owned by Gavin Ellis. He is the hotel's shooting guru and David Duguid its fisherman – so there is no shortage of local knowledge for the sporting guest.

**HOW TO GET THERE** Fly to Inverness and take a train or hire car to Forres. The hotel is situated one mile off A940 south of Forres.

Loch Lomond Golf Club, Rossdhu House, Luss, Dunbartonshire G83 8NT
**Tel** 01436 655555 **Fax** 01436 655500
**e-mail** info@lochlomond.com **website** www.lochlomond.com

**NO OF ROOMS** 23.

**COST** Only House Members can enjoy the sporting pursuits and facilities at Loch Lomond Golf Club. Membership, available from 1 October to 30 April, costs £1,500, of which £200 is an administration fee and £1,300 a levy used against accommodation, sporting pursuits, food and beverages – with the exception of golf. House members may bring guests to the club.

**FOOD** Fine dining available in the evenings. Informal dining available all day in the Spike bar. Exceptional wine list based around a Mâcon-Villages '95 House white wine and a Crozes-Hermitages '95 House red wine. The club has its own malt whisky – the Loch Lomond malt.

**SPORT ON OFFER/THAT CAN BE ARRANGED** Fishing for rainbow trout in the hotel's own stocked loch. Pike fishing in Rossdhu Bay. Salmon fishing on the Rivers Tay and Teith. Driven pheasant-shooting on Luss estates. Grouse-shooting, stalking, clay pigeon shooting and boating.

**SEASONS/BEST TIMES FOR SPECIALIST SPORTS** Traditional seasons.

**DOGS/CHILDREN WELCOME** Dogs not encouraged as there are no kennel facilities. Children over 12-years-old welcome.

**ANY OTHER INFO** Rossdhu House, an 18th-century mansion, was once the ancestral home of the Clan Colquhoun. It sits on a wooded peninsula, guarded on three sides by the banks of Loch Lomond. The club, which has an international membership, has been designed for those who expect and enjoy the very highest standards and service.

**HOW TO GET THERE** Take M8 from Glasgow Airport towards Greenock and Erskine Bridge. Exit M8 at M898 and continue over Erskine Bridge (toll 60p). Take the left exit to A82 Crianlarich. Continue north on A82 to the club's golf course. Pass the course and turn right at the sign to Luss. Turn right at the entrance gate.

Lochboisdale Hotel, Isle of South Uist, Western Isles HS8 5TH
**Tel** 01878 700332 **Fax** 01878 700367
**Star ratings** ***Scottish Tourist Board

**NO OF ROOMS** 18.

**COST** From £36.50 per person per night bed and breakfast. Weekly rates: 1 April to 7 May from £47 per person per night, dinner, bed and breakfast; 8 May to 23 September from £57 per person per night dinner, bed and breakfast; 24 September to 31 October from £52 per person per night dinner, bed and breakfast.

**SPECIAL BREAKS/OFFERS** Please enquire.

**FOOD** Traditional Scottish food, specialising in fish, seafood and game. A la carte menu and daily specials.

**SPORT ON OFFER/THAT CAN BE ARRANGED** Wild brown trout, sea-trout and salmon on South Uist's lochs. No bag limit. Lets by the week. Gillies available for £35 a day. Brown trout fishing free 1 April to 31 May; 1 June to 30 September £25 a boat. Sea-trout and salmon £35 a boat 1 July to 15 July; £55 a boat 17 July to 9 September; £35 a boat 11 September to 23 September; £30 25 September to 31 October. Also golf.

**SEASONS/BEST TIMES FOR SPECIALIST SPORTS** Brown trout: 1 April to 30 September. Best times May, June, July and early August. Salmon: July to 15 October.

**DOGS/CHILDREN WELCOME** Yes.

**ANY OTHER INFO** Lochboisdale is a small family-run sporting hotel situated at the ferry terminal overlooking the harbour with views across the Mich to Canna and Rhum. It is situated on a deeply indented sea loch on the south east of South Uist.

**HOW TO GET THERE** Sail from Oban and Mallaig to Lochboisdale as well as Uig to Lochmaddy. Daily flights from Glasgow to Benbecula.

Lochmaddy Hotel, Isle of North Uist, Western Isles HS6 5AA
**Tel** 01876 500331 **Fax** 01876 500210
**Star ratings** **AA

**NO OF ROOMS** 15.

**COST** From £35 per night bed and breakfast for a single room. From £65 per night bed and breakfast for a double room.

**SPECIAL BREAKS/OFFERS** Ten per cent discount on stays lasting seven nights or more.

**FOOD** Seafood and game feature heavily on the restaurant and bar menus. Good selection of wines and an impressive selection of malt whiskies.

**SPORT ON OFFER/THAT CAN BE ARRANGED** Salmon, sea-trout, brown trout on many lochs and sea pools. Gillies and 20 boats available. Sea angling from the hotel's own cruiser. Red deer stalking. Wildfowling for snipe, woodcock, duck and geese.

**SEASONS/BEST TIMES FOR SPECIALIST SPORTS** Traditional seasons.

**DOGS/CHILDREN WELCOME** Yes.

**ANY OTHER INFO** Lochmaddy is a traditional white-washed Highland building which overlooks the sea loch Loch Nam Madadh, which is one of Scotland's three Marine Special Areas of Conservation. Balranald is a RSPB reserve where the corncrake has a stronghold. Rod room and drying facilities. Les Routiers recommended.

**HOW TO GET THERE** By ferry via the Isle of Skye, Harris or Oban. By air from Benbecula.

Milton Park Hotel, Dalry, Castle Douglas, Kirkcudbrightshire DG7 3SR
**Tel** 01644 430286 **Fax** 01644 430655 **e-mail** lpl@easynet.co.uk
**Star ratings** Awaiting inspection.

**NO OF ROOMS** 18.

**COST** From £27.50 per person per night bed and breakfast based on two people sharing a double room. Single supplement £7.50.

**SPECIAL BREAKS/OFFERS** From £37.50 dinner, bed and breakfast per person per night based on two people sharing (minimum two-night stay).

**FOOD** All fresh local ingredients. Trout from own loch. Smoked fish and meat from local smokery. Lamb, beef and seafood a speciality. About 25 wines on wine list.

**SPORT ON OFFER/THAT CAN BE ARRANGED** Driven pheasant and wildfowling on local estates. Stalking on local estates and Forestry Commission land. Wild brown and rainbow trout on the hotel's own Loch Earlstoun. Coarse fishing on Loch Ken.

**SEASONS/BEST TIMES FOR SPECIALIST SPORTS** Traditional seasons.

**DOGS/CHILDREN WELCOME** Yes.

**ANY OTHER INFO** Milton Park affords a very secluded setting on the lochside but is not remote. There are 15 acres of garden, lawns and woodland surrounding the hotel. It was once the Sinclairs' family house and the hotel is still owned by Lord Sinclair. The house is a mixture of late Georgian, late Victorian and early Edwardian architecture.

**HOW TO GET THERE** The hotel is half a mile north west of St John's town of Dalry on A713.

Monachyle Mhor Hotel, Balquhidder, Lochearnhead, Perthshire FK19 8PQ
**Tel** 01877 384622 **Fax** 01877 384305 **website** www.monachylemhor.com
**Star ratings** ***AA

**NO OF ROOMS** 10.

**COST** From £50 per night bed and breakfast for a single room. From £70 to £90 per night bed and breakfast for a double room.

**FOOD** Scottish with French influence. Fresh, seasonal local produce used from a 40-mile radius. Venison and grouse sourced off the estate. The hotel has its own organic garden supplying fruit, vegetable and herbs. About 80 bins offered on the wine list. Awarded two AA rosettes. Recommended by *Which? Good Food Guide*.

**SPORT ON OFFER/THAT CAN BE ARRANGED** Grouse-shooting and red deer stalking on the estate. Salmon, brown trout and char fishing from Lochs Voil and Doine.

**SEASONS/BEST TIMES FOR SPECIALIST SPORTS** Traditional seasons.

**DOGS/CHILDREN WELCOME** Dogs not allowed in rooms. Children over 12-years-old.

**ANY OTHER INFO** This hotel is part of a 2,000-acre estate owned by the Lewis family. The house looks out over Lochs Voil and Doine. Friendly atmosphere. One of Britain's Top 50 Hotels. Recommended by *Which? Hotel Guide*.

**HOW TO GET THERE** From Edinburgh/Glasgow: 11 miles past Callander on A84 heading north, turn right to Kingshouse/Balquhidder. Hotel is six miles up the road.

Ossian Hotel, The Brae, Kincraig, Kingussie, Inverness-shire PH21 1QD
**Tel** 01540 651242 **Fax** 01540 651633
**e-mail** ossian@ic.scotland.net **website** www.kincraig.com/ossian.htm

**NO OF ROOMS** Nine.

**COST** From £22 to £31 per person per night bed and breakfast.

**SPECIAL BREAKS/OFFERS** Reduction for three days. Further reduction of £2 per night when dinner is taken in the hotel. Off-season rates in November.

**FOOD** Extensive à la carte menu prepared by chef/owners Johnny and Lynn Rainbow. Also café bar in the grounds for morning coffee, lunch and bar meals. Large choice of malt whiskies and wines.

**SPORT ON OFFER/THAT CAN BE ARRANGED** Fishing for salmon and trout on Loch Insh with hotel boat, £15 per rod per day. Bank fishing on Rivers Spey and Feshie, £10 per rod per day. Watersports on Loch Insh. Stalking on nearby estates. Skiing at Aviemore and golf nearby.

**SEASONS/BEST TIMES FOR SPECIALIST SPORTS** Fishing: from February to October. Stalking: September, October and November.

**DOGS/CHILDREN WELCOME** Dogs welcome. Children up to seven-years-old free; eight- to 14-years-old £8 per night; and 14 years and over £10 per night.

**ANY OTHER INFO** The Ossian Hotel is situated on the shores of Loch Insh and commands magnificent views of the Cairngorms. Ospreys often seen fishing Loch Insh while the surrounding marshes well known for holding abundant bird life.

**HOW TO GET THERE** From south take A9 to Kingussie, then B9152 to Kincraig. Turn right at the war memorial and the hotel is on the left down the Brae.

Park House, Drumoak, Banchory, Kincardineshire AB31 5AD
**Tel** 01334 839218 **Fax** 01334 839503
**e-mail** info@park-leisure.co.uk **website** www.park-leisure.co.uk

**NO OF ROOMS** Seven.

**COST** Fishing: from £7,537 for one week for six rods including meals, drink and accommodation. Driven shooting: 120- to 150-bird days for up to eight guns £23.50 per bird plus £145 for dinner, bed and breakfast per person. Extra person sharing room charged at £110.

**SPECIAL BREAKS/OFFERS** August: Park Country Sports Academy. October: Park Autumn Motor Tour. March/April: Champagne Fishing. November: Black Powder Weekend. Please enquire.

**FOOD** Traditional Scottish fare using fresh local produce. Comprehensive cellar with emphasis on Bordeaux and Burgundy wines. John Foster's interest in champagne, New World finds and pudding wines is apparent. The estate has its own malt whisky.

**SPORT ON OFFER/THAT CAN BE ARRANGED** Salmon, sea-trout and grilse fishing on Park House's 12 beats of the River Dee. Gillies and tuition available. Entirely catch-and-release. Driven pheasant-shooting at Park House. Small driven- and rough-shoots at Leuchars estate. Black Powder weekend with muzzle-loading driven days on 4 and 5 November. Roe deer stalking. Grouse-shooting on local estates. Clay pigeon shooting. Also tennis, cycling, billiards, garden golf and puff billiards.

**SEASONS/BEST TIMES FOR SPECIALIST SPORTS** Traditional seasons.

**DOGS/CHILDREN WELCOME** No dogs except for shooting parties when they must be kept in cars. Children over 12-years-old with adult supervision and by prior arrangement.

**ANY OTHER INFO** Park, a Grade A listed house, is not a guest house/hotel but the home of John Foster and his family since 1946. It is let on an exclusive basis. John also races classic cars and his wife Clarinda is Joint Master of the Fife Foxhounds. Sporting trophies adorn walls downstairs with a gigantic North American wapiti head dominating the main staircase. During the 1999 fishing season over 450 salmon and 140 sea-trout were caught at Park. Also tennis court, billiards room and a tackle/gun/drying room.

**HOW TO GET THERE** Twelve miles west of Aberdeen on the north Deeside road

Pittodrie House Hotel, Chapel of Garioch, Inverurie, Aberdeenshire AB51 5HS
**Tel** 01467 681444 **Fax** 01467 681648
**e-mail** info@pittodrie.macdonald-hotels.co.uk **website** www.macdonald-hotels.co.uk
**Star ratings** ***AA

**NO OF ROOMS** 27.

**COST** From £85 per night bed and breakfast for a single room. From £105 per night bed and breakfast for a double room.

**SPECIAL BREAKS/OFFERS** Activity breaks. Please enquire.

**FOOD** Fresh local produce used wherever possible. Specialities include game, fresh and smoked fish and Aberdeen Angus beef. Vegetables and herbs grown in hotel's own walled garden. Nearly 200 bins on the wine list and 130 malt whiskies on offer. Member of Taste of Scotland. Awarded an AA rosette.

**SPORT ON OFFER/THAT CAN BE ARRANGED** Pheasant-shooting on local estates. Roe deer stalking at Pittodrie. Clay pigeon shooting at Pittodrie. Salmon, sea-trout and brown tout fishing on the Rivers Deveron and Don. Tuition and gillies available. Also off-road driving, archery, grass buggies and squash.

**SEASONS/BEST TIMES FOR SPECIALIST SPORTS** Traditional seasons.

**DOGS/CHILDREN WELCOME** Very welcome.

**ANY OTHER INFO** Pittodrie dates from 1480 and has been the Smith family's home for over a century. The hotel is run by Theo Smith and his family portraits still grace the walls. The house is set within a 2,000-acre estate. Squash courts. Billiards room.

**HOW TO GET THERE** Pittodrie is off A96 Aberdeen to Inverness road. Two miles past Inverurie turn off for Balquhain/Chapel of Garioch.

Priory Hotel, The Square, Beauly, Inverness-shire IV4 7BX
**Tel** 01463 782309 **Fax** 01463 782531
**e-mail** reservations@priory-hotel.com **website** www.priory-hotel.com
**Star ratings** ***AA/****Scottish Tourist Board

**NO OF ROOMS** 36.

**COST** From £45 per night bed and breakfast for a single room. From £42 per person per night bed and breakfast based on two people sharing a double room.

**SPECIAL BREAKS/OFFERS** Weekends: from £42.50 per person per night dinner, bed and breakfast in a single or double room from October to April.

**FOOD** Traditional Scottish fare prepared using fresh local products. Extensive wine list and large selections of malt whiskies.

**SPORT ON OFFER/THAT CAN BE ARRANGED** Salmon and brown trout fishing on the River Beauly. Game-shooting on local estates. Also watersports, climbing and golf.

**SEASONS/BEST TIMES FOR SPECIALIST SPORTS** Traditional seasons.

**DOGS/CHILDREN WELCOME** Yes.

**ANY OTHER INFO** This is a moderately new hotel which has recently been refurbished.

**HOW TO GET THERE** Twelve miles north west of Inverness on A9 situated in the centre of Beauly.

Saplinbrae House Hotel, Old Deer, Mintlaw, Peterhead, Aberdeenshire AB42 4LP
**Tel** 01771 623515 **Fax** 01771 624472
**e-mail** enquiries@saplinbrae.co.uk **website** www.saplinbrae.co.uk
**Star ratings** ***Scottish Tourist Board

**NO OF ROOMS** Seven.

**COST** From £55 per person per night bed and breakfast for single occupancy. From £66 per night bed and breakfast for a double/twin room.

**SPECIAL BREAKS/OFFERS** From £75 per couple per night weekend dinner, bed and breakfast.

**FOOD** Both bar and brasserie. Local produce used when possible. Member of Taste of Scotland. Comprehensive wine list. Wide range beers and malt whiskies on offer.

**SPORT ON OFFER/THAT CAN BE ARRANGED** Trout fishing at the back of the hotel at Pitfour Fishery. This 37-acre lake is modelled on the Serpentine in London. Salmon and sea-trout fishing on the Rivers Ugie and Ythen. Pheasant-, pigeon- and goose-shooting on local estates. Stalking on local estates. Also golf, windsurfing, riding clay pigeon shooting and archery.

**SEASONS/BEST TIMES FOR SPECIALIST SPORTS** Traditional seasons.

**DOGS/CHILDREN WELCOME** No pets in hotel, but welcome in kennels. Children welcome.

**ANY OTHER INFO** Saplinbrae was built in 1756 as a dower house for the Fergusons at Pitfour estate. This country house is now owned and run by Julia and Andy Brown who took over the hotel in 1997. Cedar Lodge house is ideal for parties or larger groups requiring basic bunk house type accommodation at competitive rates.

**HOW TO GET THERE** Approximately 30 miles from Aberdeen. Take A92 from Aberdeen to Peterhead and Fraserburgh. At Toll of Birness turn left for Fraserburgh on A952. At the roundabout in Mintlaw turn left on to A950 New Pitsligo road. Hotel is 1½ miles on the right.

Seafield Lodge Hotel, Woodside Avenue, Grantown-on-Spey, Morayshire PH26 3JN
**Tel** 01479 872152 **Fax** 01479 872340
**e-mail** enquiries@seafield-lodge-hotel.co.uk **website** www.seafield-lodge-hotel.co.uk
**Star ratings** ****AA

**NO OF ROOMS** 14.

**COST** From £32 per person per night bed and breakfast for a double room based on two people sharing.

**SPECIAL BREAKS/OFFERS** Certain times of the year, usually November and February.

**FOOD** Innovative menus based on fresh local produce. Speciality game, venison and salmon. Both restaurant and bar meals. Extensive range of malt whiskies and fine ales.

**SPORT ON OFFER/THAT CAN BE ARRANGED** Salmon fishing on the River Spey as well as the Tulchan and Castle Grant beats. Tuition and gillies available. Stalking on local estates. Also clay pigeon shooting, off-road driving, skiing, curling, bird-watching and golf.

**SEASONS/BEST TIMES FOR SPECIALIST SPORTS** Fishing: 11 February to the end of August.

**DOGS/CHILDREN WELCOME** By prior arrangement.

**ANY OTHER INFO** Sporting talk is *de rigueur* in this hotel's bar which is hardly surprising considering the Spey runs by the hotel and the Cairngorms dominate the view. This is also the centre for Arthur Oglesby's Spey angling courses.

**HOW TO GET THERE** Take A9 to Inverness. Turn off for Aviemore then follow signs to Grantown-on-Spey.

Taychreggan Hotel, Kilchrenan, Taynuilt, Argyll PA35 1HQ
**Tel** 01866 833211 **Fax** 01866 833244
**e-mail** info@taychregganhotel.co.uk **website** www.taychregganhotel.co.uk
**Star ratings** ***AA/****Scottish Tourist Board

**NO OF ROOMS** 19.

**COST** From £99 per night dinner, bed and breakfast for a single room. From £82.50 per person per night dinner, bed and breakfast based on two people sharing a double room.

**SPECIAL BREAKS/OFFERS** Please enquire.

**FOOD** Fresh, local produce used where possible. Seafood and beef are specialities. Five-course table d'hôte dinner. Extensive wine list. Large selection of malt whiskies. Member of the Scotch Beef Club. Awarded two AA rosettes.

**SPORT ON OFFER/THAT CAN BE ARRANGED** Salmon, brown trout, rainbow trout, pike, char and perch fishing on Loch Awe and River Awe. Shark, tope, skate, conger, pollack, ling and winter cod fishing off the *Lady Jayne* on the Sound of Mull, Firth of Lorne, Coll, Tiree and Colonsay. Stalking and rough-shooting locally. Clay pigeon and laser clay shooting. Also watersports, golf, riding, gliding and microlighting.

**SEASONS/BEST TIMES FOR SPECIALIST SPORTS** Traditional seasons.

**DOGS/CHILDREN WELCOME** Dogs welcome by prior arrangement. No children under 14-years-old.

**ANY OTHER INFO** Over 300 years ago, Taychreggan was a cattle drovers' inn. The hotel is now set within 40 acres of garden and woodland on the shores of Loch Awe. Recommended by *The Good Food Guide* and *The Good Hotel Guide.*

**HOW TO GET THERE** The hotel is 88 miles from Glasgow airport. Take A85 at Taynuilt near Oban on to B845 to Kilchrenan.

The Brown Trout Hotel, Watten, Wick, Caithness KW1 5YN
**Tel** & **Fax** 01955 621354

**NO OF ROOMS** Six.

**COST** From £20 to £35 per person per night bed and breakfast.

**FOOD** Home-cooked meals. Flexible mealtimes to suit fishermen.

**SPORT THAT CAN BE ARRANGED** Salmon and trout fishing on Rivers Thurso and Wick. Wild brown trout fishing on Loch Watten. Wildfowling can be arranged. Boat hire is arranged on a daily or weekly basis with or without motor.

**SEASONS/BEST TIMES FOR SPECIALIST SPORTS** Traditional seasons.

**DOGS/CHILDREN WELCOME** Dogs by prior arrangement. Families very welcome.

**ANY OTHER INFO** The Brown Trout is run by Iain MacKenzie and his family. Garage and drying room facility.

**HOW TO GET THERE** Follow A9 from Inverness to Thurso. Watten is between Wick and Thurso.

The Carnegie Club, Skibo Castle, Clashmore, Dornoch, Sutherland IV25 3RQ
**Tel** 01862 894600 **Fax** 01862 894601
**e-mail** skibo@carnegieclubs.com **website** www.carnegieclub.co.uk

**NO OF ROOMS** 47 including lodges on estate.

**COST** Members: £275 per person per night; guest of member £325 per person per night; guest £375 per person per night. Based on two people sharing a double room. Single supplement £125 per person per night. Daily charge covers everything. Annual membership £3,000. Non members may stay at the Carnegie Club once, at the guest rate. Membership mandatory for further visits. All prices do not include VAT.

**FOOD** Traditional country-house style meals taken at one table like a dinner party. All food is fresh and local. Vegetables and fruit grown in greenhouses on the estate. Seafood a speciality. Extensive wine selection. Members store their own wine in the cellar. Selection of Scottish whiskies.

**SPORT ON OFFER/THAT CAN BE ARRANGED** Own 18-hole championship links course free to guests staying. Also a nine-hole parkland course for members only. Salmon fishing on the Beauly, Shin and Evelix. Wild brown trout fishing on Loch Ospisdale. Deep sea fishing. Pheasant-shooting on local estates. Also clay pigeon shooting, archery, off-road driving, riding, falconry and swimming.

**SEASONS/BEST TIMES FOR SPECIALIST SPORTS** Traditional seasons.

**DOGS/CHILDREN WELCOME** Yes.

**ANY OTHER INFO** Skibo is the former home of Andrew Carnegie, the Scottish-born American steel tycoon and philanthropist who left home when 13 years old and went on to to become one of the richest and most successful men of his generation. His visitor's book reads like *Who's Who*: King Edward VII, the Rockerfellers, Rudyard Kipling, Edward Elgar, Lloyd George and Helen Keller. The club's ideal is to afford superb comfort, fine cuisine, sporting activities and appropriate hospitality synonymous with being a house guest of Andrew Carnegie in the grand Edwardian era. The club was bought by Peter de Savary in 1995 and has two Outposts, one is Stapleford Park and the other 69, Cadogan Gardens. The castle is set within a 7,500-acre estate and was famously described as "Heaven on Earth" by Andrew Carnegie. Traditional butler service. Extensive unheated greenhouses provide fruit and flowers for the castle. Two home farms also supply the castle with fresh produce. Original furniture and memorabilia remain within the castle. Original marble indoor swimming pool. Also gym, tennis court, sauna and steam rooms, Clarins spa and beauty. Own stables.

**HOW TO GET THERE** Train/air to Inverness. From Inverness: A9 toward Wick. After Tain cross Dornoch Firth Bridge and take the second left on to A949 to Bonar Bridge and Lairg. In middle of Clashmore village turn left to Skibo Castle.

The Castle Hotel, Huntly, Aberdeenshire AB54 4SH
**Tel** 01466 792696 **Fax** 01466 792641
**e-mail** castlehot@enterprise.net **website** www.castlehotel.uk.com
**Star ratings** ***AA

**NO OF ROOMS** 19. Two ground-floor rooms.

**COST** From £58 per night bed and breakfast for a single room. From £42.50 per person per night bed and breakfast in a double/twin room.

**SPECIAL BREAKS/OFFERS** From £65 for a single and from £55 per person in a twin/double for three nights or more including dinner (£18 allowance), bed and breakfast. Winter rates: from £50 for a single room; £35.50 per person for a double room.

**FOOD** Local produce with game featuring heavily on the menu. Restaurant and bar menus. Well-stocked wine cellar.

**SPORT ON OFFER/THAT CAN BE ARRANGED** The hotel has its own beat on the River Deveron for salmon and trout fishing. Prices on application. Further fishing can be arranged on the Rivers Spey, Dee and Don. Pheasant-, grouse-, partridge-, duck-, woodcock- and snipe-shooting can be arranged locally as well as red and roe deer stalking. Rabbit-shooting everywhere. Hawking, golf, tennis courts, Nordic skiing and pony trekking.

**SEASONS/BEST TIMES FOR SPECIALIST SPORTS** Traditional seasons.

**DOGS/CHILDREN WELCOME** Yes.

**ANY OTHER INFO** This 18th-century building was originally known as Sandston when it was built as the family home for the Dukes of Gordon. It was extended using stone from the ruins of Huntly Castle in 1769 and renamed Huntly Lodge. Today it has strong ties with the countryside and welcomes guests wishing to enjoy fieldsports in the area.

**HOW TO GET THERE** Huntly is on A96 between Inverness and Aberdeen. From Huntly follow signs to Huntly Castle and then continue to the hotel entrance.

The Craigellachie Hotel, Speyside, Banffshire AB38 9SR
**Tel** 01340 881204 **Fax** 01340 881253
**e-mail** info@craigellachie.com **website** www.craigellachie.com
**Star ratings** ****Scottish Tourist Board

**NO OF ROOMS** 26.

**COST** From £95 per night bed and breakfast for a single room. From £115 per night bed and breakfast for a double room.

**SPECIAL BREAKS/OFFERS** Please enquire

**FOOD** Local fresh produce in modern Scottish style. Wine list offers over 200 bins. Quaich Bar with over 300 different single malts available. Awarded two AA rosettes and Hotel Bar of the Year. Member of Taste of Scotland.

**SPORT ON OFFER** Salmon fishing on the River Spey on the Ballindalloch and Rothiemurchus estates. Brown trout fishing on local lochs, the Glen of Rothes Trout Fishery and Rothiemurchus estate. Pheasant-shooting on the Ballindalloch estate. Stalking on the Glenrinnes estate. Also clay pigeon shooting, riding and golf.

**SEASONS/BEST TIMES FOR SPECIALIST SPORTS** Fishing: February to September.

**DOGS/CHILDREN WELCOME** Yes.

**ANY OTHER INFO** The Craigellachie Hotel, built in 1893, is the only hotel in Scotland that was purposely built as a hotel during that period. It sits within its own grounds and commands views over the River Spey. The Speyside Walk passes along the side of the hotel. It is very popular with guests interested in malt whisky.

**HOW TO GET THERE** From Aberdeen: A96 to Huntly then on to Inverness. Turn left to Dufftown on A920. In Dufftown take A941 to Craigellachie. From Inverness: A96 to Elgin. A941 to Craigellachie. From Perth: A9 to Aviemore. A95 to Grantown on Spey. Follow signs to Craigellachie.

The Creggans Inn, Strachur, Argyll PA27 8BX
**Tel** 01369 860279 **Fax** 01369 860637
**e-mail** info@creggans-inn.co.uk **website** www.creggans-inn.co.uk
**Star ratings** ***AA

**NO OF ROOMS** 17.

**COST** From £49 per person per night bed and breakfast in a single or double room. From £65 per person per night bed and breakfast for a superior loch-view double room.

**SPECIAL BREAKS/OFFERS** Off-season breaks: from £63 per person dinner, bed and breakfast in a standard double room. From £80 per person dinner, bed and breakfast for a loch-view double room. Minimum two-night stay between November and March.

**FOOD** In the restaurant and bar there is an emphasis on fresh local produce especially seafood and lamb and beef from neighbouring farms. Extensive wine list. Selection of rare malt whiskies. Awarded an AA rosette and a wine award 1998.

**SPORT ON OFFER/THAT CAN BE ARRANGED** Pheasant- and woodcock-shooting in Strachur Park. Stocked brown trout fishing on estate's own lochan. Salmon and sea-trout fishing on the River Ecke and other local rivers. Also sea fishing, off-road driving and archery.

**SEASONS/BEST TIMES FOR SPECIALIST SPORTS** Fishing: May to October. Local rivers are mostly spate rivers so are dependent on rainfall.

**DOGS/CHILDREN WELCOME** Yes

**ANY OTHER INFO** The Creggans Inn is situated on the shores of Loch Fyne. It was the winner of *The Sunday Times* Golden Pillow award 1999.

**HOW TO GET THERE** Glasgow to Loch Lomond, A83 and then A815 to the inn. Or, by Gourock take the car ferry across the Clyde to Dunoon and then on to A815.

The Dowans Hotel, Aberlour, Banffshire AB38 9LS
**Tel** 01340 871488 **Fax** 01340 871038 **e-mail** penny@thedowans.freeserve.co.uk

**NO OF ROOMS** 19.

**COST** From £59 per person per night bed and breakfast for a single room. From £44 per person per night bed and breakfast for a double/twin room based on two people sharing.

**SPECIAL BREAKS/OFFERS** From £520 per person weekly dinner, bed and breakfast for a single room. From £415 per person weekly dinner, bed and breakfast for a double/twin room based on two people sharing.

**FOOD** Home-cooked Scottish country house food. Flexible meal times for those involved in country sports. Comprehensive wine list. Excellent selection of malt whiskies.

**SPORT ON OFFER/THAT CAN BE ARRANGED** Salmon fishing on the River Spey. Stocked brown and rainbow trout fishing on a local fishery. Roe stalking near Glenfiddich and Dufftown. Driven pheasant-, grouse- and partridge-shooting between Aviemore and Cullen. Driven partridge on a grouse moor. Rough pigeon- and rabbit-shooting locally.

**SEASONS/BEST TIMES FOR SPECIALIST SPORTS** Salmon: March to September. Roe: May.

**DOGS/CHILDREN WELCOME** Yes and no charge.

**ANY OTHER INFO** The Dowans Hotel is owned and run by Penny and Peter Neep. It is situated within three acres of landscaped gardens which feature a large coi carp pond. Peter is a keen shot and both he and Penny fish. They are very sympathetic to guests who forget the time when fishing. The bar is known as the best "holding pool" on the Spey.

**HOW TO GET THERE** One hour from either Aberdeen or Inverness airport by car.

The Eskdale Hotel, Market Place, Langholm, Dumfriesshire DG13 0JH
**Tel** & **Fax** 01387 380357 **e-mail** hotel@eskdale.globalnet.co.uk
**Star ratings** **AA

**NO OF ROOMS** 15.

**COST** From £34 per night bed and breakfast for single room. From £54 per night bed and breakfast for a double/twin room. From £68 per night bed and breakfast for a family room.

**SPECIAL BREAKS/OFFERS** Please enquire.

**FOOD** Both table d'hôte and à la carte menus on offer in the restaurant. Bar meals also available. Choice of 36 wines.

**SPORT ON OFFER/THAT CAN BE ARRANGED** Salmon and sea-trout fishing on the Rivers Esk and Liddle. Game-shooting on the Buccleuch estate. Also golf and tennis.

**SEASONS/BEST TIMES FOR SPECIALIST SPORTS** Traditional seasons.

**DOGS/CHILDREN WELCOME** Yes.

**ANY OTHER INFO** The Eskdale Hotel is a former coaching house now run by Linda and Norman Gormley. It's a popular meeting place during the Langholm Common Riding held every summer.

**HOW TO GET THERE** Langholm is on A7, 20 miles north of Carlisle.

The Gleneagles Hotel, Auchterarder, Perthshire PH3 1NF
**Tel** 01764 662231 **Fax** 01764 662134
**e-mail** resort.sales@gleneagles.com **website** www.gleneagles.com
**Star ratings** *****AA Red

**NO OF ROOMS** 222.

**COST** From £190 per night bed and breakfast for a single room. From £280 per night bed and breakfast for a double room.

**SPECIAL BREAKS/OFFERS** Special interest programmes throughout the year: golf, riding, shooting, falconry, off-road driving and spa treatments. Also at Christmas, Hogmanay and Easter. Please enquire.

**FOOD** Fine dining in the Strathearn restaurant, Mediterranean-style cuisine at the Club or hearty golfers' fare at the Dormy Clubhouse. The bar reflects the style of great ocean liners.

**SPORT ON OFFER/THAT CAN BE ARRANGED** Salmon and sea-trout fishing on two beats of the River Tay. Rainbow and brown trout fly-fishing on the estate's lochs. Three championship golf courses. Equestrian centre featuring two indoor arenas, a BHS cross-country course and carriage-driving facilities. Also falconry. Charges: golf £85 per round in the summer and £60 per round in the winter. Off-road driving from £160 for two people. Falconry tuition in handling birds and moorland hawking from £59. Salmon, rainbow and brown trout fishing from £50. Clay pigeon, rifle-shooting and archery from £50. Riding from £33. Two swimming pools, three tennis courts, squash, snooker, gym and cycling.

**SEASONS/BEST TIMES FOR SPECIALIST SPORTS** Traditional seasons, otherwise year round.

**DOGS/CHILDREN WELCOME** Yes.

**ANY OTHER INFO** Gleneagles lies in an 850-acre estate. It was built by the former Caledonian Railway Co but is now owned by Diageo. The Spa offers beauty and therapeutic treatments such as hydrotherapy, aromatherapy, facials and massages. Also hair salon, golf shops, equestrian centre shop, shooting and fishing shop and garden nurseries.

**HOW TO GET THERE** From the south: the M9 becomes A9 (dual carriageway) at Dunblane. Continue on A9 for about 11 miles. Turn off on to A823 signed Crieff and Gleneagles and follow signs to the hotel. Hotel entrance on the left a mile farther on. From the north: leave A9 for A823, after the exit to Gleneagles Station. Turn right on to A823.

The Killiecrankie Hotel, By Pitlochry, Perthshire PH16 5LG
**Tel** 01796 473220 **Fax** 01796 472451
**e-mail** enquiries@killiecrankiehotel.co.uk **website** www.killiecrankiehotel.co.uk
**Star ratings** **AA/****Scottish Tourist Board

**NO OF ROOMS** 10.

**COST** From £88 per person per night dinner, bed and breakfast for a single or double room.

**SPECIAL BREAKS/OFFERS** From £66 per person per night dinner, bed and breakfast in November and December excluding Christmas and New Year.

**FOOD** Scotland's larder with imagination. Specialises in fish, game and beef. Wine list extends to 70 bins and 24 malt whiskies are on offer. Member of the Scotch Beef Club and Taste of Scotland. Awarded two AA rosettes.

**SPORT ON OFFER/THAT CAN BE ARRANGED** Pheasant-shooting for about £280 per day on Urrard estate. Red stag stalking for between £300 to £350 a day on Dalnacardoch estate. Roe and hind stalking on local estates. Salmon fishing on the River Garry for between £25 and £35 per rod per day. Brown trout fishing on the Rivers Garry, Tummel and Tilt, as well as local lochs.

**SEASONS/BEST TIMES FOR SPECIALIST SPORTS** Pheasant-shooting: November and December. Stalking: stags 1 July to 20 October; hinds 21 October to 31 December.

**DOGS/CHILDREN WELCOME** Both, but prefer dogs!

**ANY OTHER INFO** The Killiecrankie is a small country hotel just on the pass of Killiecrankie. It is run by the Anderson family and is renowned for its peace and quiet.

**HOW TO GET THERE** Off A9 between Pitlochry and Blair Atholl on B8079.

The Newton Hotel, Inverness Road, Nairn, Highland IV12 4RX
**Tel** 01667 453144 **Fax** 01667 454026
**e-mail** rooms@morton-hotels.com **website** www.morton-hotels.com
**Star ratings** ****AA

**NO OF ROOMS** 57.

**COST** From £80 to £95 per night bed and breakfast for a single room. From £102 to £135 per night bed and breakfast for a double room.

**SPECIAL BREAKS/OFFERS** Please enquire.

**FOOD** Fresh local produce, especially seafood, game and beef. Extensive wine list. Selection of malt whiskies. Member of Taste of Scotland. Awarded an AA rosette.

**SPORT ON OFFER/THAT CAN BE ARRANGED** Salmon, sea- and brown trout fishing on the Rivers Nairn and Findhorn. Pheasant-, pigeon-, hare-, grouse-, rabbit-, woodcock- and snipe-shooting and stalking and wildfowling on the Cawdor estate. Golf locally.

**SEASONS/BEST TIMES FOR SPECIALIST SPORTS** Traditional seasons.

**DOGS/CHILDREN WELCOME** Yes.

**ANY OTHER INFO** The house and farm at Newton has belonged to a line of families since the 1600s. It was sold as a hotel to the Sword family in 1996. During the Seventies Charlie Chaplin used to visit this hotel. He, his family and staff would take over the second floor for a few weeks each summer.

**HOW TO GET THERE** Seven miles from Inverness airport on A96 between Inverness and Aberdeen.

The Roxburghe Hotel And Golf Course, Heiton, Near Kelso, Roxburghshire TD5 8JZ
**Tel** 01573 450331 **Fax** 01573 450611
**e-mail** hotel@roxburghe.net **website** www.roxburghe.net
**Star ratings** ****AA

**NO OF ROOMS** 22.

**COST** From £120 to £255 per night bed and breakfast for a double room to include free entry to Floors Castle, use of tennis courts, croquet, bicycles and trout fishing.

**SPECIAL BREAKS/OFFERS** Golf breaks available.

**FOOD** Both table d'hôte and à la carte menus available in the restaurant. Emphasis on local game, fish and beef. Extensive wine list personally compiled by the Duke of Roxburghe. Member of a Taste of Scotland and the Scotch Beef Club. Awarded two red AA rosettes and the Scottish Tourist Board's best Light lunches/Afternoon Tea.

**SPORT ON OFFER/THAT CAN BE ARRANGED** Salmon and brown trout fishing on the estate's own beats of the Rivers Teviot and Tweed. Fly-fishing for rainbow trout in the hotel's own pond. Shooting on the estate's farms and moors. Also tennis, golf, croquet, falconry and cycling.

**SEASONS/BEST TIMES FOR SPECIALIST SPORTS** Fishing: 1 February to 1 June and 1 September to 1 December. Shooting: grouse 12 August; pheasant 1 October to 2 February.

**DOGS/CHILDREN WELCOME** Yes.

**ANY OTHER INFO** One of Scotland's finest Jacobean country houses surrounded by park and woodland. Owned by the Duke and Duchess of Roxburghe. The bedrooms are named after farms on the estate. Also on site is an Elixir Health and Beauty Clinic.

**HOW TO GET THERE** The hotel is three miles south of Kelso on A698 at Heiton.

The Royal Golf Hotel, Dornock, Sutherland IV25 3LG
**Tel** 01862 810283 **Fax** 01862 810923
**e-mail** royalgolf@morton-hotels.com **website** www.morton-hotels.com
**Star ratings** ***AA

**NO OF ROOMS** 25.

**COST** From £105 per night bed and breakfast for a double room.

**SPECIAL BREAKS/OFFERS** Please enquire.

**FOOD** Fresh local produce, especially seafood and beef. Extensive wine list. Selection of malt whiskies featured on a Whisky Wall. Member of Taste of Scotland.

**SPORT ON OFFER/THAT CAN BE ARRANGED** Salmon fishing on the River Helmsdale. Wild brown trout fishing on local lochs. Pheasant-, pigeon-, hare-, grouse-, rabbit-, woodcock- and snipe-shooting, and stalking and wildfowling on the Cawdor estate. Golf locally.

**SEASONS/BEST TIMES FOR SPECIALIST SPORTS** Traditional seasons.

**DOGS/CHILDREN WELCOME** Yes.

**ANY OTHER INFO** This hotel has had a major refurbishment this year and reopened in April. The house, set in two acres of garden, was built as a private house at the end of last century and still carries that country-house-style atmosphere. It overlooks the Royal Dornock golf course and the Dornock Firth.

**HOW TO GET THERE** One hour from Inverness. Turn off A9 just past Tain.

Tomdoun Hotel, Invergarry, Inverness-shire PH35 4HS
**Tel** 01809 511218 **Fax** 01809 511218

**NO OF ROOMS** 10.

**COST** From £22 to £26 per person per night bed and breakfast in a double/twin room based on two people sharing.

**SPECIAL OFFERS/BREAKS** For one week there is a 10 per cent discount for dinner, bed and breakfast per person.

**FOOD** Home cooking using local produce such as trout, salmon, venison and beef.

**SPORT ON OFFER/THAT CAN BE ARRANGED** Salmon, brown trout and arctic char fishing on Lochs Garry, Inch Iaggan, Poulary and 3½ miles of the upper River Garry. Brown trout fishing also on Loch Quoich. Pike fishing on Loch Loyne. Boats available. Stalking on local estates. Pony trekking and canoeing.

**SEASONS/BEST TIMES FOR SPECIALIST SPORTS** Salmon: January to October; trout: March to October. Best months May, June and September. Stalking: stags 1 July to 20 October; hinds 21 October to 15 February.

**DOGS/CHILDREN WELCOME** Yes.

**ANY OTHER INFO** The present hotel was built in 1880 to replace the original coaching inn. It was situated on the original Fort William to Skye road but when Loch Loyne was deepened the road was drowned leaving the hotel in its own peaceful location. Freezing and drying facilities for fishermen.

**HOW TO GET THERE** Turn left off A87 four miles from Invergarry. Turn left along Loch Garry to the hotel.

Tormaukin Hotel, Glendevon, By Dollar, Perthshire FK14 7JY
**Tel** 01259 781252 **Fax** 01259 781526
**e-mail** enquiries@tormaukin.co.uk **website** www.tormaukin.co.uk
**Star ratings** ***AA

**NO OF ROOMS** 10.

**COST** From £50 per night bed and breakfast for a single room. From £80 per night bed and breakfast for a double/twin room.

**SPECIAL BREAKS/OFFERS** A 10 per cent discount on stays lasting three-nights or more; 15 per cent discount on seven nights or more. Fishing packages available.

**FOOD** Large selection of international food with strong Scottish influence using local produce. Bar snacks and restaurants menus available. Over 80 bins to choose from the wine list. Recommended by Egon Ronay and *The Good Pub Guide.*

**SPORT THAT CAN BE ARRANGED** Trout fishing in local lochs. Rough- and game-shooting locally. Pony trekking and golf.

**SEASONS/BEST TIMES FOR SPECIALIST SPORTS** Fishing: March to end September.

**DOGS/CHILDREN WELCOME** Dogs by prior arrangement. Children yes.

**ANY OTHER INFO** Privately owned 18th-century drovers' inn with log fires and real ales. Renowned locally for good food and warm hospitality. One of the series of *Hooked On Fishing* with Paul Young was filmed in Glendevon naming Glensherrup as the main venue and Tormaukin Hotel as the place to stay.

**HOW TO GET THERE** From the north: leave M90 at junction 7. From south: leave M90 at junction 6. The hotel is situated on A823 between A9 and M90 in the village of Glendevon.

Traquair Arms Hotel, Traquair Road, Innerleithen, Borders EH44 6PD
**Tel** 01896 830229 **Fax** 01896 830260
**e-mail** traquair.arms@scottishborders.com
**Star ratings** ***AA

**NO OF ROOMS** 10.

**COST** From £29 per person per night bed and breakfast in a family room.

**SPECIAL BREAKS/OFFERS** From £46 per person per night dinner, bed and breakfast based on two people sharing (minimum two-night stay).

**FOOD** Modern Scottish favouring local game and salmon. Two restaurants with à la carte menus. Extensive wine list and a number of malt whiskies on offer. Members of a Taste of Scotland.

**SPORT ON OFFER/THAT CAN BE ARRANGED** Salmon fishing on Tweed. Also golf.

**SEASONS/BEST TIMES FOR SPECIALIST SPORTS** September, October and November.

**DOGS/CHILDREN WELCOME** Yes.

**ANY OTHER INFO** This hotel has recently been taken over by Gig and Dianne Johnston. The bar and restaurants have open coal fires.

**HOW TO GET THERE** M6 then M74 to Moffat. From there take A708 to Mount Benger. At the Gordon Arms turn left on to A709 to Innerleithen

Turnberry Hotel, Turnberry, Ayrshire KA26 9LT
**Tel** 01655 331000 **Fax** 01655 331706 **e-mail** turnberry@westin.com
**Star ratings** *****AA Red; RAC Blue Ribbon

**NO OF ROOMS** 132.

**COST** From £130 (low season) to from £310 (high season) per night bed and breakfast for a double/twin room based on two people sharing.

**SPECIAL BREAKS/OFFERS** Please enquire.

**FOOD** Traditional Scottish cuisine and modern lighter dining. Extensive wine list of 500 bins focusing on clarets and the New World. About 60 malt whiskies on offer.

**SPORT ON OFFER/THAT CAN BE ARRANGED** Own golf courses including the Ailsa championship course. In season game-shooting on local estates. Salmon, sea-trout, brown trout fishing arranged locally. Local gillies available for fishing on the River Girvan and Loch Doon. Stocked trout loch, shooting range, longbow and archery all available on the estate by end of year. Also heath club and spa, own tennis courts, indoor swimming pool and squash courts.

**SEASONS/BEST TIMES FOR SPECIALIST SPORTS** Traditional seasons.

**DOGS/CHILDREN WELCOME** Dogs by prior arrangement. Children welcome.

**ANY OTHER INFO** Turnberry is set within its own 800-acre estate, of which two-thirds is set aside for golf. There are plans afoot to build about 16 lodges within the estate and further expand the outdoor sporting facilities. Also sauna, solarium, steam room and beauty and hair salon. Some evenings at 6.30pm a piper can be heard outside the hotel entrance.

**HOW TO GET THERE** From Glasgow follow signs for M77/A77 towards Prestwick airport and Kilmarnock. Continue on A77 southbound through the outskirts of Ayr, Minishant, Maybole and Kirkoswald. Two miles after Kirkoswald take a right turn to Turnberry.

Longmynd Hotel, Cunnery Road, Church Stretton, Shropshire SY6 6AG
**Tel** 01694 722244 **Fax** 01694 722718
**e-mail** info@longmynd.co.uk **website** www.longmynd.co.uk
**Star ratings** ***AA

**NO OF ROOMS** 50.

**COST** From £55 per night bed and breakfast for a single room. From £50 per person per night bed and breakfast in a double room based on two people sharing.

**SPECIAL BREAKS/OFFERS** From £110 per person for two nights' dinner, bed and breakfast. From £150 per person for three nights' dinner, bed and breakfast.

**FOOD** Fresh local produce used where possible. Two-course lunch for £7.50 per person very popular. The Chapman brothers have selected 100 bins for the hotel as well as 20 half bottles.

**SPORT ON OFFER/THAT CAN BE ARRANGED** Pheasant-shooting on the Holdgate shoot. Clay pigeon and rifle-shooting on Minsterley Ranges. Hunting with the Wheatland and Wynstay Foxhounds. Brown trout fishing at two local fisheries. Coarse fishing on the River Severn. Also swimming, riding, golf and gliding.

**SEASONS/BEST TIMES FOR SPECIALIST SPORTS** Traditional seasons.

**DOGS/CHILDREN WELCOME** Dogs charged £2 per night. Children welcome.

**ANY OTHER INFO** Longmynd is situated in the South Shropshire hills. It has been owned and run by the Chapman family for three generations. During both world wars the hotel was seconded by St Dunstans for rehabilitating the war blinded. There was a hand rail built from the hotel for half a mile down the hill into Church Stretton to help the patients find their way into town. Outdoor swimming pool, sauna, solarium and gym.

**HOW TO GET THERE** A49 south of Shrewsbury. In Church Stretton turn left at Lloyds TSB, straight over mini-roundabout, first right into Cunnery Road. Hotel is on the left.

Carnarvon Arms Hotel, Dulverton, Somerset TA22 9AE
**Tel** 01398 323302 **Fax** 01398 324022 **e-mail** carnarvon.arms@virgin.net
**Star ratings** ***AA

**NO OF ROOMS** 22. Two rooms on ground floor.

**COST** From £40 per person per night bed and breakfast.

**SPECIAL BREAKS/OFFERS** Special offer for summer 2000 (until middle of August) from £25 per person per night bed and breakfast (minimum two-night stay).

**FOOD** Traditional English prepared from local produce.

**SPORT ON OFFER/THAT CAN BE ARRANGED** Hunting with nine packs on Exmoor. The hotel can recommend hirelings. Guests may bring their own horses and stable them at the hotel which will provide a livery service if required. Walked-up, driven or informal days shooting pheasant and partridge can be arranged on local estates. Clay pigeon shooting is available at a nearby shooting school. The hotel owns five miles of salmon, brown trout and grayling fishing on the Rivers Exe and Barle. Salmon fishing charges range from £20 a day from February to June up to £35 a day in September. A day's trout fishing is £10 in March to mid May and £14 from mid May to September. There is also brown and rainbow trout fishing on Wimbleball Reservoir. There are rod and drying rooms on site. Expert tuition available for fishing, shooting and riding. The West Somerset Polo Club plays on the meadow outside the hotel every Sunday during the summer. Syndicate ponies available for hire. Outdoor heated swimming pool. Billiards room.

**SEASONS/BEST TIMES FOR SPECIALIST SPORTS** Traditional seasons. Trout fishing is fly only. Best times are May to July. The dry fly is particularly effective in August. Popular flies are Black Gnat, Pheasant Tail, Tupps, Greenwell's Glory, Kite's Imperial, Blue Dun and Gold Hare's Ear.

**DOGS/CHILDREN WELCOME** Dogs charged at £4 per day and are welcome in the hotel, although kennelling is available in the stableyard. Fourteen-year-olds and under who share a room with parents are charged half the adult rate. Three-year-olds and under are charged £10.50 per night bed and breakfast.

**ANY OTHER INFO** In 1874 the 4th Earl of Carnarvon built the hotel near the banks of the River Barle to accommodate travellers arriving at the railway station.

**HOW TO GET THERE** Leave M5 at junction 27 (Tiverton). Go north following signs for Dulverton. Take B3222 to Lynmouth and the hotel is one mile farther on right.

Charlton House, Shepton Mallet, Near Bath, Somerset BA4 4PR
**Tel** 01749 342008 **Fax** 01749 346362
**e-mail** reservations-charltonhouse@btinternet.com
**Star ratings** ***AA Red

**NO OF ROOMS** 16.

**COST** From £140 per night bed and breakfast for a standard room.

**SPECIAL BREAKS/OFFERS** Please enquire about spring and summer breaks.

**FOOD** Modern English using local produce combined with international ingredients. Extensive fine wine list. Awarded three AA rosettes and a Michelin star.

**SPORT ON OFFER/THAT CAN BE ARRANGED** Clay pigeon shooting. Trout fishing on hotel's lake. Hunting with Blackmore & Sparkford Vale, Mendip Farmers Hunt and Avon Vale Foxhounds and with the Chilmark Beagles. Also golf, hot air ballooning, riding, tennis and swimming.

**SEASONS/BEST TIMES FOR SPECIALIST SPORTS** Traditional seasons.

**DOGS/CHILDREN WELCOME** Only one room available for dogs. Children welcome.

**ANY OTHER INFO** Charlton House is owned by the founders of the Mulberry label, Roger and Monty Saul. It has been restored and refurbished using the Mulberry Home Collection, antiques, paintings and quirky curios. The renowned landscaped gardens are two minutes' walk away. The Mulberry Factory shop is half a mile away. The hotel has an indoor swimming pool, tennis court, and sauna. Beauty treatments, massage and aromatherapy can be arranged.

**HOW TO GET THERE** From M4: junction 17. Take A350 and A361 toward Shepton Mallet. The hotel is one mile before Shepton Mallet on the left. From M3: junction 8. Take A303, A36 and A361 toward Shepton Mallet. Hotel is one mile before the town on the left. From M5: junction 23. Take A39 and A361 through Shepton Mallet. Hotel is one mile on the right. From A303: at Podimore turn right to Shepton Mallet. Turn right on to A361 toward Frome and the hotel is one mile on the right.

Tarr Steps Hotel, Hawkridge, Near Dulverton, Somerset TA22 9PY
**Tel** 01643 851293 **Fax** 01643 851218
**Star ratings** Recommended by *Which?* and *The Good Hotel Guide*

**NO OF ROOMS** 11.

**COST** From £65 per person per night dinner, early morning tea, afternoon tea, bed and breakfast.

**SPECIAL BREAKS/OFFERS** Seasonal offers usually available – special low season rates in July and August. Please enquire. Also has painting courses.

**FOOD** Fine English cooking using home-grown vegetables and fruit from the hotel's garden, local produce and fish from the River Barle.

**SPORT ON OFFER/THAT CAN BE ARRANGED** The hotel has 3½ miles of salmon and brown trout on the River Barle. Gillies and tuition available. Two-day fishing courses run throughout the year. Rough-shooting on 500 acres surrounding the hotel. Walked-up and driven days can be arranged with one of the many local shoots. Clay pigeon trap available. Red deer stalking is £150 a day plus from £200 for a hind and £400 to £1,000 for a stag. Hunting with Devon & Somerset Staghounds, Exmoor, Dulverton East or Dulverton West Foxhounds. Stabling available at £4.50 a day to include straw. Full livery and valeting an option. Hotel can also arrange hirelings.

**SEASONS/BEST TIMES FOR SEASONAL SPORTS** Fishing: May to September. Shooting: October to January. Stalking: stags from 1 August to 30 April; hinds 31 October to 28 February.

**DOGS/CHILDREN WELCOME** Dogs charged at £3.50 a day in the hotel or £2 a day in a kennel. Children welcome.

**ANY OTHER INFO** Tarr Steps stands in its own 11 acres of grounds and gardens. Shaun and Sue Blackmore recently revamped the hotel to the country house it once was. Fresh flowers and polished antique furniture meet you in every room. The Devon & Somerset Staghounds meet at the hotel on Armistice Day. The hotel also runs drawing and painting courses in conjunction with Monica Horn and the course's resident artist David Horn. The cost of the Landscape Course is £410 and the Getting A Likeness Course is £422. These both include five nights' dinner, bed, breakfast and packed lunch.

**HOW TO GET THERE** On the outskirts of Dulverton. In small suburb of Battleton, take the left turn signposted to Hawkridge, not Tarr Steps.

The Anchor Hotel And Ship Inn, Porlock Weir, Minehead, Somerset TA24 8PB
**Tel** 01643 862753 **Fax** 01643 862843
**e-mail** anchorhotel@clara.net **website** www.smoothhound.co.uk/hotels/anchorho.html
**Star ratings** ***AA/English Tourist Board four Crowns

**NO OF ROOMS** 20.

**COST** From £44 per person per night bed and breakfast in a double room based on two people sharing.

**SPECIAL BREAKS/OFFERS** Please enquire.

**FOOD** Anglo-French cuisine used in both table d'hôte and à la carte menus. Lobster Thermidor, and steak, kidney and oyster pies a speciality. Good wine selection. Good range of traditional ales and homemade bar meals on offer in The Ship Inn.

**SPORT ON OFFER/THAT CAN BE ARRANGED** Sea fishing. Also salmon, sea- and brown trout fishing on the River Exe. Hunting with the Devon & Somerset Staghounds and the Quantock Staghounds. Also with the Exmoor Foxhounds.

**SEASONS/BEST TIMES FOR SPECIALIST SPORTS** Traditional seasons.

**DOGS/CHILDREN WELCOME** In certain rooms. Dogs charged £4 per day. Children five- to nine-year-olds charged £17.50 per night. Ten- to 15-year-olds half adult rate.

**ANY OTHER INFO** The hotel is just 10yd from the water's edge. Recommended by Egon Ronay, Johansens and Ashley Courtenay.

**HOW TO GET THERE** From the north: take M6 then M5 to Bridgwater or Taunton junctions. Turn on to A39 to Minehead and then Porlock. From London: take M25 then M3 then A303 through Illminster to Taunton then on to A39 to Minehead and then Porlock. Follow signs to Porlock Weir for the hotel.

The Crown Hotel, Exmoor National Park, Exford, Somerset TA24 7PP
**Tel** 01643 831554 **Fax** 01643 831665
**e-mail** bradleyhotelsexmoor@easynet.co.uk **website** www.gratton.co.uk/crown
**Star ratings** ***AA

**NO OF ROOMS** 17.

**COST** From £47.50 per night bed and breakfast for a single room. From £95 to £116 per night bed and breakfast for a double room.

**SPECIAL BREAKS/OFFERS** From £56 per person per night dinner, bed and breakfast (minimum two-night or more stay).

**FOOD** Extensive and varied menus offering imaginative homemade dishes created from fresh local produce where possible. Over 60 wines on offer. Real ales. Awarded two AA rosettes.

**SPORT ON OFFER/THAT CAN BE ARRANGED** Driven- and walked-up pheasant- and partridge-shooting on local estates. Hunting with nine packs within a 25-mile radius. Fishing – please enquire.

**SEASONS/BEST TIMES FOR SPECIALIST SPORTS** Traditional seasons.

**DOGS/CHILDREN WELCOME** Yes.

**ANY OTHER INFO** The Crown Hotel is part of Exford life. It is popular with locals and visiting sportsmen alike. The hotel is owned by John Atkin and Colin Bradley who is very keen on his shooting and fishing.

**HOW TO GET THERE** Take M5 to junction 25. Follow signs for Taunton. Take A358, then B3224 via Wheddon Down to Exford.

The Exmoor White Horse Inn, Near Hendrie, Exford, Minehead, Somerset, TA24 7PY
**Tel** 01643 831229 **Fax** 01643 831246
**e-mail** exmoorwhitehorse.demon.co.uk **website** www.exmoor-hospitality-inns.co.uk
**Star ratings** **AA

**NO OF ROOMS** 26.

**COST** From £50 per person per night bed and breakfast in a double/twin room based on two people sharing. From £78 per person per night dinner, bed and breakfast.

**SPECIAL BREAKS/OFFERS** Book any two nights and get one free, meals included from £156 per person.

**FOOD** Specialises in local produce, in particular game and seafood. This hotel is famous for its pudding board. Over 50 malt whiskies on offer.

**SPORT ON OFFER/THAT CAN BE ARRANGED** Hunting with nine packs within a 25-mile radius. Fly-fishing tuition with Nick Hart. The East Lyn provides salmon, brown and sea-trout. The Rivers Barle and Exe offer brown trout and salmon fishing. Also local reservoirs. Walked-up and driven-shooting at Wellshead, Miltons and Sharcott shoots, to name a few in the area. Clay pigeon shooting. Livery stables nearby.

**SEASONS/BEST TIMES FOR SPECIALIST SPORTS** Hunting: August to the end of April. Fishing: March to the end of September. Shooting: October to the end of January.

**DOGS/CHILDREN WELCOME** Yes.

**ANY OTHER INFO** Renowned 16th-century sporting inn managed by Peter and Linda Hendrie. Just as popular with the locals as those visiting. The chat is invariably of hunting, shooting and fishing. In fact, it is a haven for those infatuated with fieldsports.

**HOW TO GET THERE** Take M5 to junction 25 (Taunton). Take B3224 to Exford.

The Hood Arms, Kilve, Near Bridgwater, Somerset TA5 1EA
**Tel** 01278 741210 **Fax** 01278 741477 **e-mail** mattbri@tinyworld.co.uk
**Star ratings** AA four diamonds

**NO OF ROOMS** Five.

**COST** From £38 per night bed and breakfast for a single room. From £52 per night bed and breakfast for a double room.

**SPECIAL BREAKS/OFFERS** One-week specials: 10 per cent discount.

**FOOD** Both the restaurant and the bar offer large and varied menus heavily featuring homemade dishes using fresh, local produce. Extensive wine list.

**SPORT THAT CAN BE ARRANGED** Hunting with Quantock Staghounds and West Somerset Vale Foxhounds. Game-shooting locally. Sea fishing from Kilve Beach. Trout fishing from Enmore, Durleigh and Wimbleball Reservoirs. Golf locally.

**SEASONS/BEST TIMES FOR SPECIALIST SPORTS** Traditional seasons.

**DOGS/CHILDREN WELCOME** Yes.

**ANY OTHER INFO** The Hood Arms is a black and white 17th-century coaching inn fronted by a cobbled yard and a coaching arch through which is a walled garden. Inside, the bars have old beams and open fireplaces. Recommended by Egon Ronay, *The Good Pub Guide* and *Which? Pub Guide.* Two self-catering cottages and a holiday flat.

**HOW TO GET THERE** Take A39 from Bridgwater towards Kilve.

The Royal Oak Inn, Withypool, Exmoor, Somerset TA24 7QP
**Tel** 01643 831506 **Fax** 01643 831659

**NO OF ROOMS** Eight.

**COST** From £37 to £46 per person per night bed and breakfast in a single or double room.

**SPECIAL BREAKS/OFFERS** Rates discounted when staying more than one night.

**FOOD** Restaurant and bar serving English cuisine prepared from fresh local ingredients. Fish popular. Selection over 70 wines and vintage ports. Exmoor Ale and Exmoor Stag brewed at Wiveliscombe. Awarded an AA rosette.

**SPORT ON OFFER/THAT CAN BE ARRANGED** Hunting with Dulverton West, Dulverton East, Exmoor Foxhounds and Devon & Somerset Staghounds. Driven and walked-up game-shooting on local estates. Brown trout and salmon fishing on the Rivers Exe and Haddeo. Rainbow trout fishing on a private lake. Clay pigeon shooting. Stabling available locally.

**SEASONS/BEST TIMES FOR SPECIALIST SPORTS** Traditional seasons.

**DOGS/CHILDREN WELCOME** Yes.

**ANY OTHER INFO** Gail Sloggett took over the Royal Oak Inn this year and has extensively refurbished it. There is plenty of history within its walls: R D Blackmore stayed here while he was writing *Lorna Doone.* When Sir Alfred Munnings stayed he painted three salmon on his bathroom wall. Fraser Smith of M15 fame used to own the pub; the James Bond character Q was based on him. Collection of memorabilia in Rod Room bar. Very popular with locals. True sporting pub. Recommended by Johansens, *Which? Good Pub Guide*, Michelin and Egon Ronay.

**HOW TO GET THERE** M5 to junction 25. A358 towards Minehead. Turn off on to B3224 towards Wheddon Cross and Exford. In Exford turn left over the bridge and follow signs to Withypool.

The Royal Oak Inn, Winsford, Exmoor National Park, Somerset TA24 7JE
**Tel** 01643 851455 **Fax** 01643 851009
**e-mail** enquiries@royaloak-somerset.co.uk **website** www.royaloak-somerset.co.uk
**Star ratings** ***AA/English Tourist Council

**NO OF ROOMS** 14.

**COST** From £85 per night bed and breakfast for a single room. From £95 per night bed and breakfast for a double room.

**SPECIAL BREAKS/OFFERS** Weekend and midweek breaks. Please enquire.

**FOOD** Both restaurant and bar meals available. English, mainly homemade and traditional. Small, select wine cellar.

**SPORT ON OFFER THAT CAN BE ARRANGED** Game-shooting on local estates. The hotel owns a mile of fishing on the River Exe. Trout fishing on Wimbleball Reservoir. Hunting with the Devon & Somerset Staghounds and the Dulverton East Foxhounds.

**SEASONS/BEST TIMES FOR SPECIALIST SPORTS** Traditional seasons.

**DOGS/CHILDREN WELCOME** Dogs charged £3.50 per dog per night. Children welcome.

**ANY OTHER INFO** The Royal Oak dates from the 12th century. It still retains many of the original features such as a thatched roof, open fires and oak beams. It is busy with locals at the weekends and is a true sporting pub.

**HOW TO GET THERE** Take M5 south, off at junction 27 to Tiverton. At the roundabout take A396 to Winsford.

The Wheelwrights Arms, Monkton Combe, Near Bath BA2 7HD
**Tel** 01225 722287 **Fax** 01225 723029

**NO OF ROOMS** Eight.

**COST** From £38 per night bed and breakfast for a single room. From £48 per night bed and breakfast for a double/twin room.

**SPECIAL BREAKS/OFFERS** Please enquire about winter breaks.

**FOOD** Homemade snacks and grills served in the bar – steaks a speciality. A la carte menu also available. Selection of real English ales. Listed in *The Good Beer Guide.*

**SPORT ON OFFER/THAT CAN BE ARRANGED** Coarse fishing on the River Avon. Riding, clay pigeon shooting and golf.

**SEASONS/BEST TIMES FOR SPECIALIST SPORTS** Summer.

**DOGS/CHILDREN WELCOME** No.

**ANY OTHER INFO** The Wheelwrights Arms was built in the middle of the 18th century and stands in the Midford Valley. It is popular with locals and well known for its beer. At one time it was in competition with the local monastery which used to brew highly recommended beer.

**HOW TO GET THERE** From Bath take A36 to Warminster. Turn left at the traffic lights. Go past the Viaduct Pub and take the first left. Go past the school and the pub is just on the left.

Gatton Manor Hotel Golf And Country Club, Standon Lane, Ockley, Near Dorking, Surrey RH5 5PQ
**Tel** 01306 627555 **Fax** 01306 627713 **e-mail** gattonmanor@enterprise.net
**Star ratings** ***AA

**NO OF ROOMS** 18.

**COST** From £67.50 per night bed and breakfast for a single room. From £52.50 per night bed and breakfast for a double/twin room. From £67.50 dinner, bed and breakfast per night based on two people sharing a double room.

**SPECIAL BREAKS/OFFERS** Please enquire.

**FOOD** British and Continental cuisine. Extensive wine list. RAC Dining award.

**SPORT ON OFFER/THAT CAN BE ARRANGED** Coarse fishing on the hotel's own lakes. Own 18-hole golf course. Two grass tennis courts.

**SEASONS/BEST TIMES FOR SPECIALIST SPORTS** Traditional seasons.

**DOGS/CHILDREN WELCOME** No dogs. Children welcome.

**ANY OTHER INFO** Gatton Manor Hotel, owned by the Heath family, was built in 1728 as a dowager house for the Abinger estate. It is set within a 200-acre estate of park and woodland and a water garden. It also has a gym, aerobics studio, sauna, jacuzzi, solarium and alternative therapists.

**HOW TO GET THERE** Take M25 junction 9. Take A24 then A29. Follow signs for the hotel.

Amberley Castle, Amberley, Near Arundel, West Sussex BN18 9ND
**Tel** 01798 831992 **Fax** 01798 831998
**e-mail** info@amberleycastle.co.uk **website** www.amberleycastle.co.uk
**Star ratings** ***AA Red

**NO OF ROOMS** 20.

**COST** From £145 to £300 per night bed and breakfast for an en-suite double room.

**SPECIAL BREAKS/OFFERS** From £380 per room for dinner, bed and breakfast for two people for two midweek nights – known as a Castle Break.

**FOOD** The 12th-century Queens Room restaurant, with its barrel-vaulted ceiling, well reflects the eclectic cuisine served here. Both table d'hôte and à la carte menus on offer. Awarded two AA rosettes.

**SPORT ON OFFER/THAT CAN BE ARRANGED** Archery, crossbow, clay pigeon shooting, falconry, riding, sea and river fishing, polo at Cowdray, sailing and golf. Also racing at Goodwood, Fontwell, Lingfield and Plumpton.

**SEASONS/BEST TIMES FOR SPECIALIST SPORTS** Traditional seasons.

**DOGS/CHILDREN WELCOME** No dogs. Children over 12-years-old welcome.

**ANY OTHER INFO** Amberley Castle has a rich history and only opened its doors to the public world in 1989 once Joy and Martin Cummings had transformed the castle into the country house hotel it is today. The Bishopric contains five suites separate from the hotel allowing late-night access without having to lower the portcullis at midnight. Each bedroom has its own jacuzzi. Licensed for civil marriages. The castle has its own colony of jackdaws whose ancestors first nested there 10 centuries ago.

**HOW TO GET THERE** Take B2139 from Storrington or Arundel. The entrance is clearly marked with Union Flag.

South Lodge Hotel, Brighton Road, Lower Beeding, Horsham, West Sussex RH13 6PS
**Tel** 01403 891711 **Fax** 01403 892289
**e-mail** enquires@southlodgehotel.co.uk **website** www.exclusivehotels.co.uk
**Star ratings** ****AA Red

**NO OF ROOMS** 41.

**COST** From £175 to £350 per night for a double room (room only).

**SPECIAL BREAKS/ OFFERS** From £115 per person per night to include accommodation, two breakfasts, two rounds of golf and one dinner (minimum two-night stay).

**FOOD** English cuisine with Mediterranean influences prepared using fresh produce from the hotel s garden and local suppliers. Library bar. Extensive wine cellar. Awarded three AA rosettes.

**SPORT ON OFFER/THAT CAN BE ARRANGED** Clay pigeon shooting. Own 36-hole golf courses. Also off-road driving, archery, tennis, riding and snooker.

**SEASONS/BEST TIMES FOR SPECIALIST SPORTS** Traditional seasons.

**DOGS/CHILDREN WELCOME** No dogs. Children welcome.

**ANY OTHER INFO** South Lodge is a Victorian country house set within 93 acres of gardens and parkland over looking the South Downs. Every effort has been made over the years to retain original features within the house such as wooden panelling and open fires.

**HOW TO GET THERE** Six miles south of Horsham on A281 towards Brighton and opposite Leonardslee Gardens.

The Spread Eagle Hotel And Health Spa, South Street, Midhurst, West Sussex GU29 9NH
**Tel** 01730 816911 **Fax** 01730 815668
**e-mail** spreadeagle@hshotels.co.uk **website** www.hshotels.co.uk
**Star ratings** ***AA

**NO OF ROOMS** 39.

**COST** From £80 per night bed and breakfast for a single room. From £110 per night bed and breakfast for double room. Charges include use of the health spa.

**SPECIAL BREAKS/OFFERS** From £49 per person per night dinner, bed and breakfast on a Sunday night – known as the Sunday Special. From £65 per person per night dinner, bed and breakfast (minimum two-night stay) during the midweek – the Midweek Special. From £75 per person per night (minimum two-night stay) at the weekend – the Weekend Break. Charges include use of the health spa.

**FOOD** Modern British style. Both à la carte and table d'hôte menus. Extensive wine list. Lunch available in the bar, courtyard, conservatory and terrace. Awarded two AA rosettes.

**SPORT ON OFFER/THAT CAN BE ARRANGED** Hunting with Chiddingfold, Leconfield and Cowdray Foxhounds. Also Cowdray Park Polo Club, golf, Goodwood and Fontwell racecourses, motor racing and Tiger Moth flying.

**SEASONS/BEST TIMES FOR SPECIALIST SPORTS** Traditional seasons, otherwise all year.

**DOGS/CHILDREN WELCOME** Yes.

**ANY OTHER INFO** The Spread Eagle Hotel is reputed to be one of England's oldest hotels and has been welcoming guests since 1430. It has an indoor swimming pool, sauna, steam room, hot tub, gymnasium and health and beauty rooms.

**HOW TO GET THERE** Take A3 from London. Follow A286 to Haslemere then Midhurst. The Spread Eagle Hotel is located in Midhurst along South Street.

Redesdale Arms Hotel, Rochester, Otterburn, Newcastle-upon-Tyne, Tyne & Wear NE19 1TA
**Tel** 01830 520668 **Fax** 01830 520063
**Star ratings** AA four diamonds

**NO OF ROOMS** 10. One room suitable for a disabled guest.

**COST** From £30 per person per night bed and breakfast based on two sharing a double room.

**SPECIAL BREAKS/OFFERS** From £95 per person for all-day riding, bed and breakfast, packed lunch and a four-course evening meal. Hunting holiday: from £153 per day to include hireling, cap, bed and breakfast and a four-course evening meal.

**FOOD** Home-cooked local produce. Recommended in the *Vegetarian Good Food Guide.* Sunday lunches a speciality.

**SPORT ON OFFER/THAT CAN BE ARRANGED** Trout fishing on the River Rede. Hotel's own hirelings are available for hunting with the Border, Jed Forest, College Valley, North Tyne, Morpeth and West Percy Foxhounds. Stables are available for guests' horses at £10 a night.

**SEASONS/BEST TIMES FOR SPECIALIST SPORTS** Foxhunting: October to April. Riding holidays all year.

**DOGS/CHILDREN WELCOME** Yes.

**ANY OTHER INFO** Redesdale Arms Hotel, an old coaching inn, is known locally as The First and Last as it was, for many years, the first and last hotel in England. It has been rebuilt and refurbished following a devastating fire in 1995. Cottage to let.

**HOW TO GET THERE** On the side of A68 between the villages of Otterburn and Rochester, 12 miles from the Border.

Caer Beris Manor Hotel, Builth Wells, Powys LD2 3NP
**Tel** 01982 552601 **Fax** 01982 552586
**e-mail** caerberismanor@btinternet.com **website** www.caerberis.co.uk
**Star ratings** ***AA/four crowns Wales Tourist Board

**NO OF ROOMS** 23.

**COST** From £51.50 per night bed and breakfast for a single room. From £41.50 per person per night bed and breakfast for a double room, based on two people sharing.

**SPECIAL BREAKS/OFFERS** From £55 per person per night dinner, bed and breakfast, based on two people sharing (minimum two-night stay). Weekend fishing breaks with Bob James and Charles Jardine from £249 per person to include instruction, meals and accommodation. From £99 dinner, bed and breakfast for the non-fishing partner who shares the accommodation.

**FOOD** Meals prepared using fresh local produce. Lighter meals served in the conservatory. Wine list features 150 bins. The bar is well stocked with cocktails reflecting the fishing theme. Many whiskies, liqueurs and beers on offer. Awarded an AA rosette.

**SPORT ON OFFER/THAT CAN BE ARRANGED** Complimentary fishing for salmon, brown trout, grayling and chub, dace, pike, shad and barbel on the River Irfon. The hotel also has guest tickets for four miles of fishing on the River Wye. Llyn Arlach and Llyn Gwyn, two well-stocked trout fisheries, are nearby. Llandrindod and Llangorse lakes offer carp, tench, perch and bream. Also Clywedog and Ponsticill Reservoirs. Tuition available with a gillie. Also clay pigeon shooting, paragliding, off-road driving, canoeing, bog snorkelling, riding and golf.

**SEASONS/BEST TIMES FOR SPECIALIST SPORTS** Salmon: October; trout: May to September; and grayling: January to March.

**DOGS/CHILDREN WELCOME** Dogs welcome. Under 16-year-olds free of charge if sharing their parents room.

**ANY OTHER INFO** Until recently, Caer Beris belonged to Lord Swansea. Now the country manor, originally built by Philip Braose in 1093, is owned and managed by Peter and Katharine Smith. It is surrounded by 27 acres of parkland and the River Irfron.

**HOW TO GET THERE** The hotel is situated on the west edge of Builth Wells on A483.

Gliffaes Country House Hotel, Crickhowell, Powys NP8 1RH
**Tel** 01874 730371/0800 146719 **Fax** 01874 730463
**e-mail** calls@gliffaeshotel.com **website** www.gliffaeshotel.com
**Star ratings** ***AA

**NO OF ROOMS** 22.

**COST** From £62 to £130 per night bed and breakfast for a double room.

**SPECIAL BREAKS/OFFERS** Between November and February off-season rates available. Please enquire.

**FOOD** Traditional with a modern Mediterranean twist. Awarded two AA rosettes.

**SPORT ON OFFER/THAT CAN BE ARRANGED** The hotel owns 2½ miles of prime wild brown trout and salmon fishing on the River Usk. Shooting parties can be arranged locally with notice. Also riding, golf, walking and cycling.

**SEASONS/BEST TIMES FOR SPECIALIST SPORTS** Fishing from 3 March to 17 October.

**DOGS/CHILDREN WELCOME** No dogs in bedrooms, but very welcome to use the stables. Children welcome.

**ANY OTHER INFO** Gliffaes has been run by the same family for 50 years. Susie and James Suter are the third generation of Brabners at Gliffaes. The hotel is set in 33 acres of gardens and woodland edging the River Usk. It has been described as "a piece of Italy with an English garden fit for a Greek god set in the Welsh hills".

**HOW TO GET THERE** Situated 1½ miles off A40 between Crickhowell and Brecon.

Lake Vyrnwy Hotel, Llanwddyn, Montgomeryshire SY10 0LY
**Tel** 01691 870692 **Fax** 01691 870259
**e-mail** res@lakevyrnwy.com **website** www.lakevyrnwy.com
**Star ratings** ****Wales Tourist Board

**NO OF ROOMS** 35.

**COST** From £110 per night bed and breakfast for a double room.

**SPECIAL BREAKS/OFFERS** Please enquire.

**FOOD** Fresh local produce used when possible. Head chef David Richards previously worked in the Ritz and Grosvenor House Hotels. His farming background has led to the hotel building up its own sheep flock to allow him and John Langfords, Welsh Butcher of the Year, the opportunity of selecting the best meat. Awarded two AA rosettes and an RAC merit award. Recommended by Johansens and *The Good Hotel* and *The Good Food Guides.*

**SPORT ON OFFER** Rainbow and brown trout fishing on three miles of the west bank of the River Vyrnwy and Lake Vyrnwy. Charged from £20 per rod per day. Driven-, walked-up and rough-shooting, charged at £22 a bird on driven days and £95 a gun on rough days. Also clay pigeon shooting, quad trekking, cycling, tennis and canoeing.

**SEASONS/BEST TIMES FOR SPECIALIST SPORTS** Fishing: 1 April to 15 October (high season 1 April to 14 July).

**DOGS/CHILDREN WELCOME** Dogs welcome at £10 per night if staying in the bedroom. Complimentary heated kennels available. Children welcome. Baby sitting can be arranged.

**ANY OTHER INFO** The Lake Vyrnwy Hotel is set within a 24,000-acre wildlife reserve 1,100ft above sea level in the Berwyn Mountains overlooking Lake Vyrnwy. The lake was developed as a reservoir to supply Liverpool and the hotel was built for the gentlemen of Liverpool to enjoy the sporting estate.

**HOW TO GET THERE** M6 to junction 10a. M54 then A5 to Shrewsbury. A458 to Welshpool then Llangadflan. Turn right on to B4395 and then left on to B4393 to Llanwddyn.

Llangoed Hall, Llyswen, Brecon, Powys LD3 0YP
**Tel** 01874 754525 **Fax** 01874 754545
**e-mail** llangoed_hall_co_wales_uk@compuserve.com **website** www.llangoedhall.com
**Star ratings** ****AA Red/*****Wales Tourist Board

**NO OF ROOMS** 23.

**COST** From £135 per night bed and breakfast for a double room on a weekday. From £155 to £315 per night bed and breakfast for a double room at the weekend.

**SPECIAL BREAKS/OFFERS** From £195 per night per double room dinner, bed and breakfast (minimum two-night stay).

**FOOD** French and British food prepared by head chef Daniel James using fresh local produce. Cellar carries over 300 wines. Awarded three AA rosettes and a Michelin star.

**SPORT ON OFFER/THAT CAN BE ARRANGED** Salmon and fly-fishing on the hotel's own beat of the River Wye (£35 per day). Gillie available. Clay pigeon shooting, off-road driving, gliding, golf and ballooning. Tennis courts on site.

**SEASONS/BEST TIMES FOR SPECIALIST SPORTS** Traditional fishing seasons, otherwise spring to autumn.

**DOGS/CHILDREN WELCOME** Dogs accommodated in heated kennels. No children under eight-years-old.

**ANY OTHER INFO** In 1880, when Llangoed consisted of 54,000 acres, the estate was won in a gambling bout by John Macnamara. Sir Clough Williams-Ellis was commissioned to redesign the house in 1912. He was convinced the house was built upon the site of Wales' legendary White Palace – then the fledgling Welsh parliament. Now Llangoed, owned by Sir Bernard Ashley, stands in 17 acres of gardens on the banks of the River Wye. Its connections with the Ashley family are apparent in the hotel's interior decoration which is complemented by historical paintings and antiques. Aromatherapy massages available. Billiards room.

**HOW TO GET THERE** On A470 10 miles south of Builth Wells, 10 miles north east of Brecon and one mile north of Llyswen.

Milebrook House Hotel, Milebrook, Stanage, Knighton, Powys LD7 1LT
**Tel** 01547 528632 **Fax** 01547 520509 **e-mail** hotel@milebrook.kc3ltd.co.uk
**Star ratings** **AA/***Welsh Tourist Board

**NO OF ROOMS** 10. Bedroom suitable for disabled use.

**COST** From £51 per night bed and breakfast for a single room. From £37.75 to £41.75 per person per night bed and breakfast based on two people sharing a double room.

**SPECIAL BREAKS/OFFERS** Two-day break: from £53.25 per person per night dinner, bed and breakfast. Three-day break: from £51 per person per night dinner, bed and breakfast. Weekly: from £45.85 per person per night for seven nights' dinner, bed and breakfast.

**FOOD** English style menu with a Continental twist. Food prepared using home-grown and local produce. Extensive wine list. Awarded an AA rosette. Named as one of the AA's Best Restaurants in Britain.

**SPORT ON OFFER/THAT CAN BE ARRANGED** Brown trout fishing on the hotel's own mile-long stretch of the River Teme. Golf locally.

**SEASONS/BEST TIMES FOR SPECIALIST SPORTS** Fishing 1 April to 30 September.

**DOGS/CHILDREN WELCOME** No dogs. Children over eight-years-old welcome.

**ANY OTHER INFO** Milebrook House is a country house hotel owned and run by Rodney and Beryl Marsden. It is set in three acres of gardens which range from herbaceous to formal to the kitchen garden which leads down to the River Teme. The house was once the home of explorer Sir Wilfred Thesiger and has been visited by Emperor Haile Selassie. Recommended by *The Good Hotel Guide*.

**HOW TO GET THERE** The hotel is two miles east of Knighton on A4113 toward Ludlow.

Palé Hall, Palé estate, Llandderfel, Bala, Gwynedd LL23 7PS
**Tel** 01678 530285 **Fax** 01678 530220
**e-mail** palehall@fsbdial.co.uk **website** www.palehall.co.uk
**Star ratings** ****Welsh Tourist Board

**NO OF ROOMS** 17.

**COST** From £47.50 to £77.50 per person per night bed and breakfast.

**SPECIAL BREAKS/OFFERS** Please enquire.

**FOOD** Seasonal table d'hôte menu using fresh local produce. Extensive wine list. Awarded two AA rosettes.

**SPORT ON OFFER/THAT CAN BE ARRANGED** Salmon, brown trout, grayling, pike and perch fishing on the hotel's stretch of the River Dee. Salmon and brown trout fishing on the River Tryweryn. Coarse fishing at Bala Lake. Driven pheasant- and partridge-shooting locally.

**SEASONS/BEST TIMES FOR SPECIALIST SPORTS** Traditional seasons.

**DOGS/CHILDREN WELCOME** No dogs. Children by arrangement.

**ANY OTHER INFO** Palé Hall is a Victorian mansion set within 150 acres of parkland on the edge of Snowdonia National Park. The house was built for Henry Robertson, a Scottish gentleman, who gave orders to spare no expense. The bath and half-tester bed used by Queen Victoria during her visit in 1889 are still in use. The house operates on water-generated electricity which has helped to keep the house's running costs down over the years and hence ensure its maintenance. It remained empty for 22 years but in 1992 was bought by Saul and Judith Nahed who renovated and restored the house. Inside, the boudoir has a hand-painted ceiling, there is a galleried staircase and marble fireplaces and bar.

**HOW TO GET THERE** Palé Hall is off B4401 Corwen to Bala road, four miles from Llandrillo.

The Bear Hotel, Crickhowell, Powys NP8 1BW
**Tel** 01873 810408 **Fax** 01873 811696 **e-mail** bearhotel@aol.com
**Star ratings** ****AA

**NO OF ROOMS** 30.

**COST** From £49.50 to £94 per night bed and breakfast for a single room. From £65 to £120 per night bed and breakfast for a double room.

**FOOD** The food is a mixture of English and French classical using fresh local produce wherever possible. Welsh lamb, salmon from the Rivers Usk and Wye and Welsh Black beef are specialities. Bistro bar offers more of the comfort foods and country-style items. Two wine lists: the good value, good drinking list where prices vary from £10 to £16 a bottle and the list Stephen Hindmarsh produces when asked. The hotel's stone cellar with its vaulted ceiling has been restored ensuring perfect conditions for beer and wine. There are three draught beers on offer alongside the guest beer. Awarded two AA rosettes.

**SPORT ON OFFER/THAT CAN BE ARRANGED** Salmon and brown trout fishing in the River Usk. Shooting on Glen Usk estate. Also golf, watersports and pony trekking.

**SEASONS/BEST TIMES FOR SPECIALIST SPORTS** Traditional seasons.

**DOGS/CHILDREN WELCOME** Yes.

**ANY OTHER INFO** The Bear Hotel is a 15th-century, black-and-white coaching inn close to the River Usk. Some bedrooms have a jacuzzi. Popular with locals. Mr and Mr Hindmarsh have been running this hotel for 24 years. Won Best Pub in Britain 2000. Recommended by Egon Ronay.

**HOW TO GET THERE** Crickhowell is on A40 between Abergavenny and Brecon.

The Bryn Morfydd Hotel, Llanrhaeadr, Near Denbigh, Denbighshire LL16 4NP
**Tel** 01745 890280 **Fax** 01745 890488
**e-mail** reception@bryn-morfydd.co.uk
**Star ratings** ***AA

**NO OF ROOMS** 30.

**COST** From £38 per person per night bed and breakfast in a single or double room. From £56 per person per night dinner, bed and breakfast (includes use of hotel golf course).

**SPECIAL BREAKS/OFFERS** Midweek: From £51 per person per night dinner, bed and breakfast including use of the hotel's golf course.

**FOOD** Both table d'hôte menu in restaurant and bar snacks. Good selection of reasonably priced wines.

**SPORT ON OFFER/THAT CAN BE ARRANGED** Brown trout fishing on Rivers Elwy, Brenig and Aled. Pheasant-shooting on the hotel's golf courses (no golf on those days). Golf on the hotel's 27-hole complex. Also pony trekking and fishing.

**SEASONS/BEST TIMES FOR SPECIALIST SPORTS** Traditional seasons.

**DOGS/CHILDREN WELCOME** Yes.

**ANY OTHER INFO** The Bryn Morfydd Hotel, owned by David and Sarah Frith, is set in over 100 acres overlooking the Vale of Clwyd between the two medieval towns of Denbigh and Ruthin.

**HOW TO GET THERE** From M6 join M56. Follow signs for A55. Follow A55 to St Asaph then join A525. The Bryn Morfydd Hotel is about 2½ miles outside Denbigh on the right.

The Griffin Inn, Llyswen, Brecon, Powys LD3 0UR
**Tel** 01874 754241 **Fax** 01874 754592
**e-mail** info@griffin-inn.freeserve.co.uk **website** www.griffin-inn.co.uk
**Star ratings** **AA/***Welsh Tourist Board

**NO OF ROOMS** Seven.

**COST** From £70 per night bed and breakfast for a double room.

**SPECIAL BREAKS/OFFERS** Special rates to Friends of The Griffin.

**FOOD** Country cooking using produce of the land, rivers and seas. The hotel's garden provides the herbs and flowers and a local estate the salad ingredients. True old-fashioned cookery – slow roasts and casseroles a speciality. Well stocked with ales. Extensive wine list. Recommended by *The Good Food Guide*.

**SPORT ON OFFER/THAT CAN BE ARRANGED** Salmon, brown trout and grayling fishing on the Rivers Wye and Edw. Driven- and walked-up pheasant-shooting on local estates. Fallow stalking in Herefordshire. Hunting with the Brecon and Golden Valley Foxhounds and Glyn Celyn Beagles.

**SEASONS/BEST TIMES FOR SPECIALIST SPORTS** Traditional seasons.

**DOGS/CHILDREN WELCOME** Prefer dogs.

**ANY OTHER INFO** The Griffin has been run by the Stockton family for four generations. The bedrooms are named after famous salmon flies. Very popular with the locals. A true sporting pub.

**HOW TO GET THERE** Llyswen is on A470 east of Builth Wells. The Griffin is on the right in the village.

Warpool Court Hotel, St David's, Pembrokeshire SA62 6BN
**Tel** 01437 720300 **Fax** 01437 720676 **e-mail** warpool@enterprise.net
**Star ratings** ***AA/****Welsh Tourist Board

**NO OF ROOMS** 25.

**COST** From £56 per person per night bed and breakfast based on two people sharing a double room.

**SPECIAL BREAKS/OFFERS** From £71 per person per night dinner, bed and breakfast based on two people sharing a double room.

**FOOD** Strong presence of fish on an imaginative menu. For example, it serves locally caught crab and sea bass. Fresh local ingredients used where possible. Extensive wine list. Awarded two AA rosettes and an RAC Food Merit Award.

**SPORT ON OFFER/THAT CAN BE ARRANGED** Sea fishing. Also riding and golf.

**SEASONS/BEST TIMES FOR SPECIALIST SPORTS** Traditional seasons.

**DOGS/CHILDREN WELCOME** Yes.

**ANY OTHER INFO** Warpool Court Hotel is privately owned by Peter Trier. The hotel has panoramic sea views over St Bride's Bay to the offshore islands of Skomer and Ramsey. Seven acres of garden.

**HOW TO GET THERE** London 270 miles; Severn Bridge 135 miles; and Carmarthen 50 miles. From the cross square in St David's, bear left and follow signs to the hotel.

Antrobus Arms Hotel, 15 Church Street, Amesbury, Salisbury, Wiltshire SP4 7EU
**Tel** 01980 623163 **Fax** 01980 622112 **website** www.antrobushotel.co.uk
**Star ratings** **AA

**NO OF ROOMS** 18.

**COST** From £50 per night bed and breakfast for a single room. From £80 per night bed and breakfast for a twin/double room.

**SPECIAL BREAKS/OFFERS** Weekend offers for two people: from £200 for Friday and Saturday nights' dinner, bed and breakfast and carvery Sunday lunch.

**FOOD** Varied and extensive menu using fresh local produce. Over 50 wines and a large range of malt whiskies on offer. Awarded an AA rosette. Les Routiers recommended.

**SPORT ON OFFER/THAT CAN BE ARRANGED** Fishing on a local stocked pond and nearby rivers. Also tennis, golf and racing at Thruxton.

**SEASONS/BEST TIMES FOR SPECIALIST SPORTS** Traditional seasons.

**DOGS/CHILDREN WELCOME** Yes.

**ANY OTHER INFO** The Antrobus Arms Hotel was built in the 17th century as the town house for a local family. It then became a school for young gentlemen. There is a walled Victorian garden. Stonehenge is less than two miles from the hotel.

**HOW TO GET THERE** From A303 head for Amesbury town centre.

Bishopstrow Hotel, Warminster, Wiltshire BA12 9HH
**Tel** 01985 212312 **Fax** 01985 216769
**e-mail** enquiries@bishopstrow.co.uk **website** www.slh.com
**Star ratings** ****AA

**NO OF ROOMS** 32.

**COST** From £195 per night bed and breakfast for a double room.

**SPECIAL BREAKS/OFFERS** Country breaks: from £110 per person in a double room for two nights' dinner, bed and breakfast.

**FOOD** Two restaurants and bar offer fresh local produce. Modern English.

**SPORT ON OFFER/THAT CAN BE ARRANGED** Clay pigeon shooting. Brown trout fishing on the hotel's own stretch of the River Wylye. Also archery, swimming, tennis, gym, golf, riding and cycling.

**SEASONS/BEST TIMES FOR SPECIALIST SPORTS** Traditional seasons.

**DOGS/CHILDREN WELCOME** Dogs charged £7.50 per night. Children charged £25 per night.

**ANY OTHER INFO** Bishopstrow Hotel, built in 1817 of Bath stone, is set within 27 acres of the Wylye Valley. It is filled with antiques, log fires and fresh flowers. The gardens have been developed over 200 years and show fine examples of rare species, as well as over 100 rose varieties. Ragdale Spa offers indoor and outdoor swimming pools and tennis courts, gymnasium, sauna, hair salon as well as health and beauty treatments. Complimentary membership to hotel guests. Hotel has its own wedding licence.

**HOW TO GET THERE** From London and M25: take M3 to junction 8 on to A303. Take A36 to Warminster. Follow signs to Warminster on B3414 and the hotel is on the right one mile before the town. From the north and south west: take M5 to junction 20. M4 east to junction 17 then A350 to Warminster. Hotel a mile outside the town on the left off B3414.

Longs Arms, Steeple, Ashton, Trowbridge, Wiltshire BA14 6EU
**Tel & Fax** 01380 870245 **e-mail** chantal@stayatthepub.freeserve.co.uk
**Star ratings** **AA

**NO OF ROOMS** Two.

**COST** From £25 per person per night bed and breakfast.

**SPECIAL BREAKS/OFFERS** Please enquire

**FOOD** Restaurant and bar snacks available. The menu has a heavy French influence and specialises in fresh fish and game (in season). The extensive wine list is exclusively French and there are a large selection of wines available by the glass. Food prepared and cooked by owners Chantal and Steve Whittell.

**SPORT ON OFFER/THAT CAN BE ARRANGED** Shooting on local farms. Trout fishing on local lakes and the River Avon. Hunting with the Avon Vale Foxhounds. Golf locally.

**SEASONS/BEST TIMES FOR SPECIALIST SPORTS** Traditional seasons.

**DOGS/CHILDREN WELCOME** Dogs by prior arrangement. Children welcome.

**ANY OTHER INFO** This is a 17th-century Bath stone old coaching house. The restaurant has a French feel and the bar a wooden floor and great atmosphere. Popular with the locals.

**HOW TO GET THERE** Off A350 near Trowbridge.

Lucknam Park Hotel, Colerne, Near Bath, Wiltshire SN14 8AZ
**Tel** 01225 742777 **Fax** 01225 743536
**e-mail** reservations@lucknampark.co.uk **website** www.luckhnampark.co.uk
**Star ratings** ****AA Red/English Tourist Board; Michelin Red Hotel four turrets

**NO OF ROOMS** 41.

**COST** From £150 per night for a single room (room only). From £190 per night for a double room (room only). Rate includes use of the Leisure Spa.

**SPECIAL BREAKS/OFFERS** From £220 per room per night du jour dinner and English breakfast – known as a Leisure Break. The Spring Champagne Break is as above but it includes a five-course dinner on the second night and champagne.

**FOOD** Menu du Jour, Classical and à la carte menus on offer in the restaurant. Light snacks available all day at the Leisure Spa. Awarded three AA rosettes.

**SPORT ON OFFER/THAT CAN BE ARRANGED** The hotel has its own equestrian centre with an all-weather arena and cross-country course. Tuition and livery service available. Also golf, local pheasant-shooting, clay pigeon shooting, cycling and tennis.

**SEASONS/BEST TIMES FOR SPECIALIST SPORTS** Traditional seasons.

**DOGS/CHILDREN WELCOME** No dogs. Children under 12-years-old not allowed in restaurant. Meals available in the Leisure Spa.

**ANY OTHER INFO** A Palladian house set in 500 acres of parkland approached by a mile-long avenue of 400 lime and beech trees planed in 1827. The walled garden houses a 19th-century dovecote as well as formal rose, lavender and herb gardens. Indoor swimming pool, sauna, whirlpool sauna, solarium, beauty salon and gymnasium. Runner-up of Best UK Spa Hotel 1999. Two floodlit tennis courts. Recommended by Johansens.

**HOW TO GET THERE** From London: leave M4 at junction 17. Take A350 to Chippenham, then A420 to Bristol for three miles. At Ford turn left toward Colerne. After three miles turn right at crossroads. Hotel entrance on right. From Bath: take A4 to Chippenham. Travel two miles to Batheaston and turn left for Colerne. At the crossroads for Colerne turn left. Hotel entrance on right. Travelling east: exit M4 at junction 18. Take A46 to Bath for three miles. At mini-roundabout turn left on to A420 for five miles. Turn right at Ford. After three miles turn right at crossroads for Colerne. Hotel entrance on right.

The Crudwell Court Hotel, Crudwell, Near Malmesbury, Wiltshire SN16 9EP
**Tel** 01666 577194 **Fax** 01666 577583
**Star ratings** None as yet but are refurbishing to *** deluxe level

**NO OF ROOMS** 15.

**COST** From £88 per night bed and breakfast for a double room.

**SPECIAL BREAKS/OFFERS** From £143 per person for two nights' dinner, bed and breakfast based on two people sharing a double room.

**FOOD** Full à la carte menu. Fresh local produce where possible. Gloucester Old Spot pork and smoked quails' eggs and salmon are specialities. Extensive wine list. Popular with shooting parties.

**SPORT ON OFFER/THAT CAN BE ARRANGED** Hunting with the Beaufort Foxhounds. Clay pigeon shooting. Go-karting and golf.

**SEASONS/BEST TIMES FOR SPECIALIST SPORTS** Traditional seasons.

**DOGS/CHILDREN WELCOME** Yes.

**ANY OTHER INFO** This hotel was taken over by Derek and Karen Woods at the end of April. The 17th-century rectory turned into a private house at the turn of the century and has been a hotel for 15 years. There are three acres of formal gardens with a Victorian ornamental pond.

**HOW TO GET THERE** M4 junction 17. Take A429 towards Cirencester. The hotel is three miles outside Malmesbury on the right.

Buckland Manor, Near Broadway, Worcestershire WR12 7LY
**Tel** 01386 852626 **Fax** 01386 853557 **e-mail** Buckland-Manor-UK@msn.com
**Star ratings** *****AA

**NO OF ROOMS** 13.

**COST** From £205 to £345 per night bed and breakfast for a double room.

**FOOD** English cuisine with a Continental influence using fresh local produce where possible. Extensive wine list and a wide selection of cognacs and vintage ports. Awarded three AA rosettes and RAC Gold Ribbon.

**SPORT ON OFFER/THAT CAN BE ARRANGED** Hunting with the North Cotswold and Heythrop Foxhounds. Pheasant-shooting on local estates. Coarse and trout fishing on local lakes. Also riding, swimming, tennis and golf.

**SEASONS/BEST TIMES FOR SPECIALIST SPORTS** Traditional seasons.

**DOGS/CHILDREN WELCOME** No dogs. Children over 12-years-old welcome.

**ANY OTHER INFO** There are records of Buckland Manor stretching back to the 7th century AD. In 600AD the Abbot of Gloucester received the house as a gift from Kynned, ruler of Mercia and the chief king of the seven kingdoms of the English nation. In the Domesday Book the manor was valued at £9. After the dissolution, the house passed into the Gresham, Thynne and Granville families. It is now owned by Roy and Daphne Vaughan who have maintained the traditional English country house atmosphere. The house is furnished with antiques and fine art. There are 11 acres of formal gardens. Tennis court. Outdoor swimming pool.

**HOW TO GET THERE** Just over one mile south of Broadway on B4632.

Hadley Bowling Green Inn, Hadley Heath, Near Droitwich, Worcestershire WR9 0AR
**Tel** 01905 620294 **Fax** 01905 620771
**e-mail** hbginn@backissues.freeserve.co.uk **website** www.english-inns.co.uk/HadleyBowlingGreen
**Star ratings** Three Crowns.

**NO OF ROOMS** 14.

**COST** From £53 to £85 per person per night bed and breakfast based on two people sharing.

**SPECIAL BREAKS/OFFERS** From £30 per person per night bed and breakfast (minimum two-night weekend stay).

**FOOD** Bar and restaurant menus. Emphasis on fresh, locally-sourced homemade meals. Comprehensive and moderately priced wine list. The pub's superb cellar conditions ensure a wide choice of hand-pumped real draught ales, draught cider and Irish stouts are on offer at the bar.

**SPORT ON OFFER/THAT CAN BE ARRANGED** Trout fishing at Woodland Fisheries which is well known for its angling competitions. Clay pigeon shooting. Also golf and bowls. The hotel, as the name suggests, is the proud owner of the oldest crown bowling green in England, dating back to 1575 when records began.

**SEASONS/BEST TIMES FOR SPECIALIST SPORTS** Traditional seasons.

**DOGS/CHILDREN WELCOME** Yes.

**ANY OTHER INFO** This inn dates back to the 16th century. It is a family-run business and is popular with the locals. To those who watched *Noah's Ark* on television this pub was the vets' local – The Melton Bowling Green Inn. It is also known as one of the meeting places of Guy Fawkes and his allies when he was planning the Gun Powder Plot.

**HOW TO GET THERE** From M5 junction 5: A38 towards Droitwich. Follow the Worcester signs on the ringroad then turn left to Ombersley and Tenbury. Follow signs to the hotel. From M5 junction 6: A449 towards Kidderminster and Worcester. At the roundabout where A449 divides, follow Kidderminster. Two miles later turn right to Hadley. The pub is one mile on the left.

The Chequers Inn, Fladbury, Pershore, Worcestershire WR10 2PZ
**Tel** 01386 860276 **Fax** 01386 861286
**Star ratings** **AA/Three Crowns English Tourist Board

**NO OF ROOMS** Eight.

**COST** From £49 per night bed and breakfast for a single room. From £60 per night bed and breakfast for a double/twin room.

**SPECIAL BREAKS/OFFERS** From £55 per night for a double/twin room (minimum two-night stay). Also golf breaks.

**FOOD** A la carte dining-room and bar snacks. Extensive and varied home-cooked menu with an emphasis on local produce especially fruit and vegetables from the Vale of Evesham. Sunday carvery a speciality. Over 27 wines offered. Real ales.

**SPORT ON OFFER/THAT CAN BE ARRANGED** Coarse fishing on the River Avon. Racing at Cheltenham, Stratford, Warwick and Worcester. Hunting with North Cotswold and Croome and West Warwickshire Foxhounds. Cricket at Worcestershire. Also golf and canoeing.

**SEASONS/BEST TIMES FOR SPECIALIST SPORTS** Traditional seasons.

**DOGS/CHILDREN WELCOME** No dogs. Children welcome.

**ANY OTHER INFO** The Chequers is privately owned and managed by brother and sister Emma and Jonathan Byrd. The main part of the pub dates back to the 14th century. Strong local trade.

**HOW TO GET THERE** Three miles from Evesham on A4538 Evesham to Pershore road in Fladbury.

The Lygon Arms, Broadway, Worcestershire WR12 7DU
**Tel** 01386 852255 **Fax** 01386 858611
**e-mail** info@the-lygon-arms.co.uk **website** www.savoy-group.co.uk
**Star ratings** ****AA Red

**NO OF ROOMS** 65.

**COST** From £110 per night bed and breakfast for a single room. From £150 per night bed and breakfast for a double room.

**SPECIAL BREAKS/OFFERS** Please enquire about the Midweek choice and the Cotswold weekend.

**FOOD** The hotel has two restaurants: The Great Hall, with its barrel-vaulted ceiling, and Oliver's Brassiere. The Cotswold Bar serves light lunches only. All menus focus on fresh local produce with fruit and vegetables from the Evesham Vale.

**SPORT ON OFFER/THAT CAN BE ARRANGED** Game-shooting on local estates. Tuition available. Clay pigeon shooting. Coarse and trout fishing on stocked lakes. Hunting with Heythrop, North Cotswold and the Cotswold Foxhounds. Hirelings available. Also carriage driving, off-road driving, tennis, swimming, golf, ballooning, cycling, gliding and watersports.

**SEASONS/BEST TIMES FOR SPECIALIST SPORTS** Traditional seasons.

**DOGS/CHILDREN WELCOME** Yes.

**ANY OTHER INFO** The Broadway parish first refers to the inn in 1532. In the 17th century it served both sides of the Civil War; Oliver Cromwell stayed here before the decisive battle of Worcester and Charles I also used the inn to meet his supporters. Being on the main coaching route between England and Wales, it was not long before the inn enjoyed prosperity. General William Lygon acquired it in the 19th century and the Savoy Group bought it in 1986. There are three acres of lawn. The bedrooms are decorated and furnished with antiques in traditional country-house style. Tennis court and indoor swimming pool. Gymnasium, solarium, steam room and spa bath. Billiards.

**HOW TO GET THERE** From London: M40 to Oxford. A40 to Burford. A242 through Stow-on-the-Wold then A44 to Broadway.

The Mill At Harvington, Anchor Lane, Harvington, Evesham, Worcestershire WR11 5NR
**Tel** & **Fax** 01386 870688
**Star ratings** **AA

**NO OF ROOMS** 21. Wheelchair access to certain bedrooms and bathrooms.

**COST** From £63 per night bed and breakfast for a single room. From £89 per night bed and breakfast for a double room.

**SPECIAL BREAKS/OFFERS** Short breaks: from £99 per night bed and breakfast for two people sharing a double room (minimum two-night stay).

**FOOD** Modern English and French with a country feel. Aim to use fresh, local seasonal produce. Light meals available on the terrace. Extensive wine list.

**SPORT ON OFFER/THAT CAN BE ARRANGED** Chub, roach, dace and barbel fishing on the hotel's own stretch of the River Avon. Also boating, swimming, tennis and golf.

**SEASONS/BEST TIMES FOR SPECIALIST SPORTS** Traditional seasons.

**DOGS/CHILDREN WELCOME** No dogs in the hotel. Children over 10-years-old welcome.

**ANY OTHER INFO** The Mill is a country house hotel set in an eight-acre garden which runs along 600ft of River Avon frontage. Originally, it was a malting mill, then used for hop drying and as a bread mill. The cast-iron bakery doors, together with many of the original wooden beams, can still be seen in the hotel. Also a heated outdoor swimming pool and a tennis court.

**HOW TO GET THERE** The Mill is not in Harvington but is reached by a bridge over A46 bypass off the Evesham to Bidford road.

The Talbot, Knightwick, Worcestershire WR6 5PH
**Tel** 01886 821235 **Fax** 01886 821060

**NO OF ROOMS** 10.

**COST** From £67.50 per night bed and breakfast for a double en-suite room.

**SPECIAL BREAKS/OFFERS** From £49.50 per person per night dinner, bed and breakfast (minimum two-night stay).

**FOOD** All locally grown and reared from the hotel's own organic garden and 700-acre farm. The Clifts have gradually worked towards an almost exclusively locally sourced and yet extensive menu. The Talbot is the only inn which brews its own beer from its own hops. It makes its own preserves, breads, black puddings and raised pies. Salads, vegetables and fruit come from the hotel's garden. Extensive wine list.

**SPORT ON OFFER/THAT CAN BE ARRANGED** Local coarse fishing. Pheasant-shooting at Lulsley. Also cycling, canoeing, golf and clay pigeon shooting.

**SEASONS/BEST TIMES FOR SPECIALIST SPORTS** Traditional seasons.

**DOGS/CHILDREN WELCOME** Yes.

**ANY OTHER INFO** The Talbot, a 15th-century black and white inn is situated on the banks of the River Teme. It is run by two sisters Annie and Wiz Clift. Brother Philip is the director of English Hops and chairman of the National Farmers' Union hops committee. Food and wine courses can be arranged locally.

**HOW TO GET THERE** From Worcester take A44 west to Leominster. About eight miles out of Worcester turn right on to B4197 towards Martley. The Talbot is 500yd along this road.

Nags Head Country Inn, Pickhill, Thirsk, Yorkshire YO7 4JG
**Tel** 01845 567391 **Fax** 01845 567212
**e-mail** reservations@nagsheadpickhill.freeserve.co.uk
**website** www.nagsheadpickhill.co.uk
**Star ratings** **AA

**NO OF ROOMS** 17 including two ground-floor rooms.

**COST** From £40 per night bed and breakfast for a single room. From £60 per night bed and breakfast for a double/twin room.

**SPECIAL BREAKS/OFFERS** Weekend break: dinner, bed and breakfast on the Friday and Saturday nights at normal rates but the third night is free of charge.

**FOOD** Dine either in the restaurant, bar or Tap room. Restaurant decorated and furnished with a library theme. Raymond Boynton presides over the food and his brother Edward the extensive wine list. Same large eclectic menu served in all three rooms. Nearly 100 wines (ranging from £10 to £500 a bottle) on offer with many interesting bin ends. Local beers featured. Recommended by Michelin and *The Good Food Guide*.

**SPORT ON OFFER/THAT CAN BE ARRANGED** Driven pheasant- and partridge-shooting on Thimbleby and Bolton estates. Coarse fishing on the River Swale. Rainbow trout fishing on lakes. Sea fishing. Hunting with Bedale and West of York. Golf, off-road driving and clay pigeon shooting. Racing at Ripon, Thirsk, Wetherby and Catterick (discounts available to hotel guests).

**SEASONS/BEST TIMES FOR SPECIALIST SPORTS** Shooting during season. Fishing in season. Golf and riding year round.

**DOGS/CHILDREN WELCOME** Both welcome but only with well-behaved owners!

**ANY OTHER INFO** Brothers Edward and Raymond Boynton have presided over The Nags Head since 1972. This 200-year old coaching inn is in the heart of James Herriot country. Edward is a keen horseman and has his own point-to-pointers. Also a cottage available for let.

**HOW TO GET THERE** Take Masham turn off from A1 from both north and south and the village is signposted off B6267 in Ainderby Quernhow.

The Blue Lion Inn, East Witton, Near Leyburn, North Yorkshire DL8 4SN
**Tel** 01969 624273 **Fax** 01969 624189 **e-mail** bluelion@breathemail.net

**NO OF ROOMS** 12.

**COST** From £69 to £89 per night bed and breakfast for a double room.

**SPECIAL BREAKS/OFFERS** Three nights for the price of two (excluding July and August).

**FOOD** Modern and classical English. Freshly prepared using local ingredients wherever possible. Bar meals on offer. Selection traditional hand-pulled beers. Extensive wine list. Dining Pub of the Year 1998.

**SPORT ON OFFER/THAT CAN BE ARRANGED** Brown trout and grayling fishing on the River Ure. Clay pigeon shooting. Racing at Catterick, Ripon, Wetherby and York. Tennis and pony trekking.

**SEASONS/BEST TIMES FOR SPECIALIST SPORTS** Traditional seasons.

**DOGS/CHILDREN WELCOME** Yes.

**ANY OTHER INFO** The Blue Lion was built at the end of the 18th century as a coaching inn attracting trade from drovers and travellers through Wensleydale. It is now run by Paul Klein, a keen shot.

**HOW TO GET THERE** From the south: from A1 take B6267 to Masham. Then follow A6108 past Masham to East Witton. From the north: turn off A1 at Scotch Corner and follow A6108 to Richmond and then to Leyburn. Turn left to Middleham still on A6108 to East Witton.

The Boars Head Hotel, Ripley, Near Harrogate, North Yorkshire HG3 3AY
**Tel** 01423 771888 **Fax** 01423 771509
**e-mail** boars@ripleycastle.co.uk **website** www.ripleycastle.co.uk
**Star ratings** ***AA

**NO OF ROOMS** 25.

**COST** From £95 to £115 per night bed and breakfast for a single room. From £115 to £135 per night bed and breakfast for a double room.

**SPECIAL BREAKS/OFFERS** Yorkshire break: from £75 per person based on two people sharing a double/twin room for two nights' dinner, bed and breakfast. Super Sleuth weekend: from £220 per person based on two people sharing a double/twin room, two nights' accommodation, full board and wine.

**FOOD** The hotel aims to expand the waistline and enrich the soul of guests while dining. Restaurant and traditional bistro/bar menus. Waiting staff employed for the effect of their soft French accent on the guests. Nearly 200 wines on offer. Crack shot ale is brewed for the estate to an old family recipe. Large selection of malt whiskies and cognacs. Awarded two AA rosettes.

**SPORT THAT CAN BE ARRANGED** Coarse and fly-fishing on estate lake. Days often available to guests on the estate's own syndicate shoot. Clay pigeon shooting. Laser-shooting, air-rifle and pistol-shooting. Also archery, falconry, abseiling, canoeing, off-road driving, ballooning and tennis.

**SEASONS/BEST TIMES FOR SPECIALIST SPORTS** Traditional seasons.

**DOGS/CHILDREN WELCOME** Dogs (£10 per night) allowed in bedrooms and bar. Children up to 15-years-old are charged at £20 per night.

**ANY OTHER INFO** In 1900 Ripley had three pubs. One of them, The Star Inn, was the breakfast stop for travellers making their way between Leeds and Edinburgh. When Sir William Ingilby inherited the estate he decreed all three inns should close on Sundays to prevent churchgoers from crossing the market square for further spiritual sustenance. The landlords departed and Ripley was a dry village for 71 years. Sir Thomas and Lady Ingilby opened The Boar's Head in 1990. Such was the locals' relief that the vicar came on the opening night and blessed the beer taps. Winner of the Prestigious Cesar Award in *The Good Hotel Guide* 1999. Yorkshire Tourist Board Hotel of the Year.

**HOW TO GET THERE** From the north: A1 to Ripon, then A6 towards Harrogate. Ripley is on the junction with B616. From the south: A1 to Wetherby, then A661 to Harrogate, then A61 towards Ripon. Ripley is on the junction with B616.

The Falcon Inn, Arncliffe, Skipton, North Yorkshire BD23 5QE
**Tel** & **Fax** 01756 770205

**NO OF ROOMS** Five.

**COST** From £28 per person per night bed and breakfast in a single or double room. From £35 per person dinner, bed and breakfast in a single or double room.

**FOOD** Bar food at lunch times. Three-course set evening homemade meals using fresh local produce (residents only). Real ales. Selection of wine.

**SPORT ON OFFER/THAT CAN BE ARRANGED** Wild brown trout fishing on the Falcon's own stretch of the River Skirfare. Riding locally.

**SEASONS/BEST TIMES FOR SPECIALIST SPORTS** Traditional seasons.

**DOGS/CHILDREN WELCOME** No dogs in the bar. Children welcome.

**ANY OTHER INFO** The Falcon has been run by the Miller family for 120 years. It is a small, traditional village pub popular with the locals.

**HOW TO GET THERE** From Skipton take the Grassington B6265 to Threshfield. Carry straight on towards Ketterwell then take B6160 past Kilnsey Crag. Turn left for Arncliffe just after the Crag.

The Grange Hotel, 1 Clifton, York YO30 6AA
**Tel** 01904 644744 **Fax** 01904 612453
**e-mail** info@grangehotel.co.uk **website** www.grangehotel.co.uk
**Star ratings** ***AA Red/RAC Blue Ribbon

**NO OF ROOMS** 30.

**COST** From £99 per night bed and breakfast for a single room. From £125 per night bed and breakfast for a double room.

**SPECIAL BREAKS/OFFERS** Short Breaks: from £59 per person per night for two nights' dinner, bed and breakfast based on two people sharing a double room.

**FOOD** Classic French and modern British cuisine. Fine dining in the Ivy Restaurant. Informal in the Seafood Bar and Brasserie (early suppers for theatre). Extensive wine lists. Awarded two AA rosettes. Recommended by *The Good Food Guide.*

**SPORT ON OFFER/THAT CAN BE ARRANGED** Racing in North Yorkshire. Hunting with the Sinnington, Middleton and York & Ainsty Foxhounds. Game-shooting on local estates.

**SEASONS/BEST TIMES FOR SPECIALIST SPORTS** Traditional seasons.

**DOGS/CHILDREN WELCOME** Dogs by prior arrangement. Children welcome.

**ANY OTHER INFO** This Regency-style hotel, which exudes a country-house atmosphere, is within walking distance of the Minster and holds one of York's smartest addresses. It is owned and was created by Jeremy and Vivien Cassel who used to run Capability Brown, one of London's most fashionable restaurants. Christopher Gollut, who designed the House of Lords' dining-room, helped redesign the hotel's interior. In the Seafood Bar there is a trompe-l'oeil mural of York races with the jockeys sporting the colours of some of the best names in racing.

**HOW TO GET THERE** The Grange Hotel is situated on A19 York/Thirk road and is 400yd from York city centre.

The Hawnby Hotel, Hawnby, Near Helmsley, York YO62 5QS
**Tel** 01439 798202 **Fax** 01439 798344
**e-mail** info@hawnbyhotel.co.uk **website** www.hawnbyhotel.co.uk
**Star ratings** **AA

**NO OF ROOMS** Six.

**COST** From £45 per night bed and breakfast for a single room. From £60 per night bed and breakfast for a double room.

**SPECIAL BREAKS/OFFERS** From £55 per night bed and breakfast for a double room (minimum three-night or more stay).

**FOOD** Varied and extensive menu for both restaurant and bar.

**SPORT ON OFFER/THAT CAN BE ARRANGED** Brown trout and grayling fishing on the Rivers Seph and Rye. The lake at Arden Hall is stocked with rainbow trout. Pheasant- and grouse-shooting can be arranged on Mexborough estate.

**SEASONS/BEST TIMES FOR SPECIALIST SPORTS** Traditional seasons.

**DOGS/CHILDREN WELCOME** Dogs can be kept in kennels in village. Children welcome.

**ANY OTHER INFO** The Hawnby Hotel is a traditional country inn independently owned and run. The restaurant has magnificent views over the valley. Real fires in the bar. Warm hospitality.

**HOW TO GET THERE** From south: take M1 to A1 to A19 to A170 to Scarborough and Thirsk. Follow signs for Sutton bank. After a roundabout signposted for Sutton Bank take the left-hand road for Boltby and Felixkirk. Eight miles over the moors drop into Hawnby. There is a map with directions on the hotel's website.

The Sportsmans Arms Hotel, Wath-in-Nidderdale, Pateley Bridge, Harrogate, North Yorkshire HG3 5PP
**Tel** 01423 711306 **Fax** 01423 712524
**website** www.nidderdale.co.uk
**Star ratings** **AA

**NO OF ROOMS** 13.

**COST** From £45 to £50 per night bed and breakfast for a single room. From £40 to £50 per person per night bed and breakfast in a double room, based on two people sharing.

**SPECIAL BREAKS/OFFERS** From £80 per person dinner, bed and breakfast for a two-night stay from November to March – known as a Winter Midweek Break.

**FOOD** Fresh English with French flavour. Fresh fish from Whitby daily. Local lamb, beef and pork. Game in season – grouse a speciality. Bar and restaurant menus. Extensive wine list. Selection of vintage ports, brandies, malt whiskies and liqueurs.

**SPORT ON OFFER/THAT CAN BE ARRANGED** Grouse-shooting on Swinton, Dallowgill, Middlesmoor, Longside, Heathfield, Scar, Stean and Wath moors – to name a few. Fishing on the hotel's own stretch of the River Nidd. Wild brown trout on nearby Gouthwaite Reservoir.

**SEASONS/BEST TIMES FOR SPECIALIST SPORTS** Traditional seasons.

**DOGS/CHILDREN WELCOME** No dogs in rooms, kennels available nearby. Children welcome but there are no family rooms.

**ANY OTHER INFO** Situated in a completely unspoilt village in an Area of Outstanding Natural Beauty, The Sportsmans Arms sits close to the River Nidd and is managed by Jane and Ray Carter. This 17th-century hostelry can only be reached by a pack horse bridge and is renowned locally for its warm hospitality.

**HOW TO GET THERE** Take the Pateley Bridge turning off B6265 between Ripon and Grassington. Come off A59 on to the Harrogate B651 and then turn off for Pateley Bridge.